A Prayer Companion Journal

for the

Narcissistic Abuse Survivor's Soul

Heal Your Golden Heart,

and

Be Self~Confident AGAIN!

by

Beverly Banov Brown, M.S.

OTHER BOOKS
BY
BEVERLY BANOV BROWN, M.S.

CHILDREN'S BOOKS
Windflyer

Illustrated by Hannah Handel

NON~FICTION BOOKS

A Prayer Companion Journal for the
Inspired Entrepreneur's Soul

A Prayer Companion Journal for the
Spiritual Seeker's Soul

A Prayer Companion Journal for the
Empowered Woman's Soul

If You Are Struggling
with
CoDependency,
Narcissistic Abuse,
Energy Vampires,
Marital Issues,
Self ~Rejection,
Financial Hardships,
Authentic Dating,
Overcoming Limited Beliefs,
and Inner Peace,

Beverly Banov Brown, M.S.
Hosts a YouTube Channel,
Where She Discusses These
Topics and More.

DEDICATION

A PRAYER COMPANION JOURNAL
FOR THE NARCISSISTIC ABUSE
SURVIVOR'S SOUL
IS RESPECTFULLY DEDICATED
TO ALL OF US
WHO HAVE EVER ENDURED
THE DEVASTATION
OF NARCISSISTIC ABUSE,
YET VALIANTLY CHOOSE TO HEAL
AND EVOLVE
INTO
WISER, MORE VIBRANTLY
LOVING SOULS.

MAY EACH PRAYER IN THIS BOOK
INSPIRE,
REINVIGORATE,
COMFORT,
SOOTHE
AND HELP US
TO FIND DEEPENING
PROSPERING FAITH.

A Prayer Companion Journal
for the
Narcissistic Abuse
Survivor's Soul

Watercolor/Acrylic Painting
by
Beverly Banov Brown, M.S.

Illustrations and Book Design
by
Hannah Handel

Feel free to get in touch with either
Beverly Banov Brown, M.S.
or
Hannah Handel
at
yourtranscendencecoach@gmail.com
or
coachhq@gmail.com

Published by Your Transcendence Now LLC

Your suggestions for new topics are always welcome.

Never hesitate to be in touch, as we continue this lifelong journey together co-creating a

LIVING LEGACY OF LOVE.

In Light and Wholeness,
Beverly Banov Brown, M.S.

yourtranscendencecoach@gmail.com
or
coachhq@gmail.com

TABLE OF CONTENTS

A Prayer Companion Journal
for the
Narcissistic Abuse Survivor's Soul

Introduction/Invitation

Dear Fellow Abuse Survivor,
**The Entire Prayer Companion
Journal series**
is ideal for use in 12 step recovery programs,
as well as
in
Groups,
Spiritual Organizations
and
Individual Use.

From the glossary on narcissistic behaviors,
to the loving tone on each page,
this book is **your** invitation
to solidifying a
deeper,
closer
Walk
with the
God
of your understanding.

May the Prayers
in this interactive
**Prayer Companion Journal
for the Narcissistic Abuse
Survivors Soul**,
(the 4th in
The Prayer Companion Journal series
already published are:

**A Prayer Companion Journal for the
Inspired Entrepreneurs Soul,**

**A Prayer Companion Journal for the
Spiritual Seekers Soul**

and

**A Prayer Companion Journal
for the Empowered Woman's Sou**l)
gracefully guide your recovery process.

Though you're free to read the prayers
in sequence,
or,
use the book to answer
general questions

about your own healing journey,
such as,
which qualities are most important
in reclaiming your
strength,
self-respect,
self-compassion,
ability to recover strong trust in yourself
to make great new choices,
heal from rejection,
lies,
sarcasm,
broken dreams,
physical,
mental,
financial,
spiritual
abuse,
renew your
health,
wealth,
purpose,
family ties,
enlarge your circle of friends,
etc...

Please,
trust that you are being guided
to the ideal prayer for that exact need.
Using the open-ended questions,
which follow every prayer,
you're encouraged to
write,
journal,
draw,
doodle,
cartoon,
sing,
paint,
dance,
sculpt,
move,
walk
to express your ever-evolving
emotions,
faith,
capacity
to renew your connection to
joy,
love,
respect,
fulfillment,

**prosperity
and
grace.**

Having personally
endured a variety of abuses,
including Narcissistic Abuse,
has allowed me profound compassion,
and heightened insight,
as I've had the sacred privilege
of working with
thousands of survivors.

**As an Intuitive Healer/Personal and
Business Coach,**
and as an
Interfaith Chaplain
(Founding Director since 1997
of a free,
nondenominational Prayer Network
called
The LightBridge Interfaith Prayer
Community)
for nearly 40 years,

I know the extraordinary power
of prayer
to cause holy,
inner and outer,
shifts.

We become able
to heal,
be blessed,
and prospered
as we actively **choose** new, **smoother paths**
and **kinder, wiser relationships,**
We learn
to know our own
indwelling
worth,
dignity,
beauty
and
resilience
fully.

Our presence becomes more of a gift
to everyone in our world
automatically.

As I write this Introduction/Invitation
for you,
I am putting the finishing touches
on the two next books
in this series,

**A Prayer Companion Journal for the
Recovering Codependents Soul.**

Codependent's are frequently major targets
of
Narcissistic Personalities,
so these
Prayer Companion Journals
may be used separately or together.

Also nearing completion is
**A Prayer Companion Journal for the
Intuitive Empath's Soul-**
Another group who are frequently favorites
of Narcissistic Personalities' attentions.

Please feel free to contact me with accounts
of answered prayer,
interest in doing a

Full Consultation,
by phone,
or,
with ideas
for new topics
in the
Prayer Companion Journal Series,
which will be of upliftment
and use
for you.

My **YouTube Channel,**
Beverly Banov Brown, M.S.
has several hundred videos on
**Narcissistic Relationships,
Codependency Revealed,
Radical Gratitude,
Authentic Dating,
Inner Peace Now,
About Vanishing Twin Syndrome,**
etc...

Thank you for
your
**courage,
determination
and resiliency**
in transcending

**the devastation
of Narcissistic,
and the many other forms of,
abuse.**

I am proud and grateful to walk this path
alongside you as we co-create a more
consistently loving world.

In Faith and Love,
Beverly Banov Brown, M.S.

yourtranscendencecoach@gmail.com
and
coachhq@gmail.com

CHAPTER 1
HEALING
AND
INSIGHTFUL
LESSONS
WHICH
LIBERATE.

MORNING PRAYER
TO
EMBRACE
HEALING AND RENEWAL,
NOW.

Gracious and Loving Spirit,
I am choosing
to be in the state of gratefulness
for this new day.

**I AM CHOOSING TO FOCUS ON WHAT IS
WONDERFUL,
RICH,
CREATIVE,
NURTURING,
GENEROUS,
AMAZING
AND TRULY LOVING
IN MY LIFE.**

**THANK YOU, SPIRIT,
FOR MY HEALTH,
WISDOM,
WEALTH,
LEISURE,
CARING FRIENDS,
FAMILY,
HOME, ETC..**

20

Your unending supply of
air,
sunlight,
water
and wind,
all allow for the continuation of life
on this sacred earth.

**MAY EVERY ACTION I TAKE BE ROOTED
IN AN AWARENESS OF THE BLESSINGS
I MAY FORMERLY HAVE TAKEN FOR GRANTED.**

Every single moment of each day,
miracles of healing and renewal
are happening.

I am so awake to the endless possibilities
as I move past old habits,
eliminate untrue ideas from my mind,
and embrace anew my deepening awareness
of the Love You Are.

All is in Divine Right Order.

Thank You, Thank You, Thank You!

How Does This Prayer Apply to Your Life Right Now?

What Emotions and Dreams Does This Bring Up for You?

HOW WOULD YOU MODIFY THIS PRAYER IN YOUR OWN WORDS?

USING THIS PRAYER, WHAT IS ONE STEP YOU CAN DO TO TRANSFORM THE ABUSE YOU'VE ENDURED?

WHO HAVE BEEN
YOUR MOST INSPIRING
TEACHERS IN THIS LIFETIME?
HOW MIGHT THEY RESPOND
TO THIS PRAYER?
WHAT WOULD THEY SHARE
TO SUPPORT YOUR
HEALING PROCESS?

Reassurance
for
My Inner Child.

There is a secret language
Divine Love
speaks.

Holy Spirit,
whisper to my beleaguered **INNER CHILD**,
"Never give up on your dreams.
I am always with you no matter where
you go,
no matter who else accompanies you."

Can that be so?

I've thought so often in my doubt and fear
of being inadequate,
not smart enough,
wise enough,
funny enough,
attractive enough,
lovable or loving enough...

ASSIST ME IN HEARING YOU MORE CLEARLY, LORD!

I yearn to discard ancient doubts which sometimes topple my deep desire to sense Your Eternal Embrace!

A smoother road needs to be revealed.

Little child of my inner realms, be patient and trust the protection which has brought us this far, and will always lead us home to a warm, welcoming heart.

Thank You,
Spirit,
Thank You.

How Does This Prayer Apply to Your Life Right Now?

What Emotions and Dreams Does This Bring Up for You?

How Would You Modify This Prayer in Your Own Words?

Using This Prayer, What is One Step You Can Do to Transform the Abuse You've Endured?

WHO HAVE BEEN
YOUR MOST INSPIRING
TEACHERS IN THIS LIFETIME?
HOW MIGHT THEY RESPOND
TO THIS PRAYER?
WHAT WOULD THEY SHARE
TO SUPPORT YOUR
HEALING PROCESS?

Purification and Transcendence.

I am in the process of
devouring ancient error thoughts
and messages.

Their lack-based,
fear instilling,
limitation lifestyle
no longer feels like home
to me.

I am recognizing the
Presence of the Divine Feminine
everywhere abundant
in my body,
and Spirit.

**I AM VIEWING
DIVINITY
WITHIN EVERYONE
AND EVERYTHING
MY LIFE TOUCHES.**

This Presence,
which I am,
illuminates each new message of
empowered living with hope,
strength,
optimism,
dynamic visions of a pleasing present,
an unlimited future of
good,
joy,
love,
plenty and wisdom.
My life is so much greater than error
messages can accommodate.

**I AM GIVING THANKS
FOR THIS PURIFICATION PROCESS
WHICH GENTLY RELAUNCHES**

MY LIFE
IN
HAPPIER DIRECTIONS.

Blessings abound.

Joy predominates

PEACE,
LOVE,
LAUGHTER,
EMBRACE MY LIFE,
AND I AM WHOLLY HEALED
RIGHT HERE,
RIGHT NOW!

I am grateful beyond measure.

How Does This Prayer Apply to Your Life Right Now?

What Emotions and Dreams Does This Bring Up for You?

How Would You Modify This Prayer in Your Own Words?

Using This Prayer, What is One Step You Can Do to Transform the Abuse You've Endured?

WHO HAVE BEEN
YOUR MOST INSPIRING
TEACHERS IN THIS LIFETIME?
HOW MIGHT THEY RESPOND
TO THIS PRAYER?
WHAT WOULD THEY SHARE
TO SUPPORT YOUR
HEALING PROCESS?

PRAYER TO HEAL
HAVING BEEN
UNFAIRLY BLAMED.

I have been involved
with a blameshifter,
Lord.

I hate being unjustly
accused,
demeaned,
disrespected...

Reconnect me
to my innate sense
of fairness
and inner harmony,
please.

I've allowed another's opinion
to become more significant
than my own.

Never a good plan,
is it?

**THIS SITUATION REQUIRES
A CHANGE OF PERCEPTION
ON MY PART
SO I CAN
INVITE,
ALLOW,
AND ACT
ON DIVINE GUIDANCE.**

I am willing to change
any and all attitudes
which could hold me back,
tie me
to old messages
of
limit and lack.

There are more than enough ways
that I can heal and recover
my full dignity,
know my God-given talents
and use them effectively

in the service
of myself,
and others,
in service to the One Presence
and Power
active in and through all...
God.

The sweetness of Life
which enables us to thrive
doesn't have room for
relationships
where lack of respect
predominates.

I know the truth of this now.

**I AM GRATEFUL FOR
POWER RECLAIMED,
FREEDOM CHERISHED,
AND THE VERY REAL CHANCE
TO THINK AS NEVER BEFORE,
ASSURED.**

**THANK YOU,
HOLY SPIRIT,
FOR LOVING ME
NO MATTER WHAT.**

Amen.

HOW DOES THIS PRAYER APPLY TO YOUR LIFE RIGHT NOW?

WHAT EMOTIONS AND DREAMS DOES THIS BRING UP FOR YOU?

HOW WOULD YOU MODIFY
THIS PRAYER IN YOUR
OWN WORDS?

Using This Prayer,
What is One Step
You Can Do
to
Transform the Abuse
You've Endured?

WHO HAVE BEEN
YOUR MOST INSPIRING
TEACHERS IN THIS LIFETIME?
HOW MIGHT THEY RESPOND
TO THIS PRAYER?
WHAT WOULD THEY SHARE
TO SUPPORT YOUR
HEALING PROCESS?

No One's Scapegoat Anymore!

I am taking heart from the declaration
I have been guided to adopt:
I AM NO ONE'S SCAPEGOAT ANYMORE!

There is no longer anyone whose
judgments,
opinions,
criticisms,
or even,
compliments,
I will choose to put above
the inner compass of loving guidance I
receive from inside
my soul.

**NO ONE KNOWS ME BETTER
THAN THE
DIVINE PRESENCE.**

**NO PERSON,
THING,
PLACE**

**OR GROUP
HAS THE RIGHT TO DEFINE ME.**

Like a wall of protection,
my faith becomes an unwavering
shield which cannot be violated ever
again by the pressures of this world.

**I AM FUELED BY DIVINE SOURCE,
AND ALL IS WELL
ALL THE TIME.**

Amen.

How Does This Prayer Apply to Your Life Right Now?

What Emotions and Dreams Does This Bring Up for You?

How Would You Modify This Prayer in Your Own Words?

Using This Prayer, What is One Step You Can Do to Transform the Abuse You've Endured?

WHO HAVE BEEN
YOUR MOST INSPIRING
TEACHERS IN THIS LIFETIME?
HOW MIGHT THEY RESPOND
TO THIS PRAYER?
WHAT WOULD THEY SHARE
TO SUPPORT YOUR
HEALING PROCESS?

EMPATHY FOR OTHERS
CAN ONLY GET
OUT OF BALANCE
WHEN I FORGET
TO FIRST
GIVE UNDERSTANDING
TO MY OWN
NEEDS,
WANTS,
AND
DREAMS.

Had I taken my own needs
totally for granted
in matters of
body,
mind,
and emotions
for too long?

**HAD I SHUNTED ASIDE
MY MOST FERVENT ASPIRATIONS
TO DO THE BIDDING
OF OTHERS
WHO MAY HAVE FELT
IT WAS
THEIR RIGHT
TO INSIST ON IT ALL
BEING DONE
THEIR WAY?**

Has my
emotional,
spiritual,
financial and/or physical well-being
been damaged by all of this?

What am I prepared to do
after **OVER-EMPATHIZING**
for so long?

Remind me,
Lord,
as Your Child,
I serve no one well
when I forget my care

must be
the first priority
AFTER my love
for You.

Only when I keep refilling
my well,
can I healthily offer
comfort,
support,
and guidance
to
anyone else.

A hard lesson,
I am learning.

Life evolves.

Thy Will be done.

How Does This Prayer Apply to Your Life Right Now?

What Emotions and Dreams Does This Bring Up for You?

How Would You Modify This Prayer in Your Own Words?

USING THIS PRAYER, WHAT IS ONE STEP YOU CAN DO TO TRANSFORM THE ABUSE YOU'VE ENDURED?

WHO HAVE BEEN
YOUR MOST INSPIRING
TEACHERS IN THIS LIFETIME?
HOW MIGHT THEY RESPOND
TO THIS PRAYER?
WHAT WOULD THEY SHARE
TO SUPPORT YOUR
HEALING PROCESS?

INSTRUCT ME, GOD, HOW TO FULLY LOVE MYSELF BETTER.

I need a time
FOR
SELF-NURTURING,
Lord.

A TIME AND SPACE
WHERE OLD PATTERNS
WHICH TAUGHT ME THAT
MY OWN
HEALTH,
WELL-BEING,
PEACE,
PROSPERITY,
LOVE
AND

**AND CAREER
CAN BE
RECTIFIED.**

They cannot come
before my own well-being
filled to the brim,
and an abundance
and renewal
of Light
that I can be,
that I was born to be.

**INSTRUCT ME,
GOD,
HOW TO FULLY
LOVE MYSELF.**

Whether it's the mattress I sleep on,
or the food and beverages
which fuel my Body Temple,
the home I dwell in
reflecting my self-esteem
in its spaciousness
and cleanliness,
the books I read,

the films I watch,
the songs I listen to
the work I devote myself to,
the relationships I dedicate
my caring heart to
- it is all of significance.

It is part of me giving back
to You
for the gift of life
You've afforded me.

May I never take any blessing
for granted,
even for a moment,
ever again.

Amen.

How Does This Prayer Apply to Your Life Right Now?

What Emotions and Dreams Does This Bring Up for You?

How Would You Modify This Prayer in Your Own Words?

USING THIS PRAYER, WHAT IS ONE STEP YOU CAN DO TO TRANSFORM THE ABUSE YOU'VE ENDURED?

WHO HAVE BEEN
YOUR MOST INSPIRING
TEACHERS IN THIS LIFETIME?
HOW MIGHT THEY RESPOND
TO THIS PRAYER?
WHAT WOULD THEY SHARE
TO SUPPORT YOUR
HEALING PROCESS?

PRAYER
FOR
HEALING DESPAIR.

Is there a lost and found
for
discarded dreams?

Help me rediscover
my original innocence
and passion
for
living the dreams
of my heart,
Lord.

Discarded hopes
seem to have
crushed
my natural buoyancy,
my inborne joy.

I dislike feeling,
at times,
like discouragement,
and,
even despair,
can take up residence
in my
tired mind.

Like an uninvited visitor,
whose presence
is no longer welcome,
despairing attitudes must vacate
the property of
my plans,
my thoughts,
and
my life.

Thank You,
Holy Spirit,
for working yet another miracle
within my system
which eradicates

those shattering inner voices
of the past
from family,
societal messages,
advertising,
negative relationship rejections
and letdowns.

**THERE IS NO SPACE
IN MY HEART
FOR ANYTHING
UNLIKE
DIVINE LOVE,
MOMENT TO MOMENT,
BECAUSE I AM NOW WILLING
TO REMEMBER WHOSE CHILD
I AM.**

This Truth changes
despair to hope,
depression
to
upliftment.
MY PEACE IS ASSURED.

Thanks is given.

HOW DOES THIS PRAYER APPLY TO YOUR LIFE RIGHT NOW?

WHAT EMOTIONS AND DREAMS DOES THIS BRING UP FOR YOU?

How Would You Modify This Prayer in Your Own Words?

USING THIS PRAYER, WHAT IS ONE STEP YOU CAN DO TO TRANSFORM THE ABUSE YOU'VE ENDURED?

WHO HAVE BEEN
YOUR MOST INSPIRING
TEACHERS IN THIS LIFETIME?
HOW MIGHT THEY RESPOND
TO THIS PRAYER?
WHAT WOULD THEY SHARE
TO SUPPORT YOUR
HEALING PROCESS?

I Am
Pledging
Allegiance
to the
Purity
of
My Essential Soul.

For so long
I pledged allegiance
to the
will of other's
needs,
prejudices,
fears
and
manipulations.

Those days are gone.

The dead past must be buried.

I am replacing
old,
misguided
thoughts,
attitudes,
and
rationalizations
because
**A BETTER WAY
IS MY
BIRTHRIGHT.**

So,
here I am,
hand on heart,
**PLEDGING
ALLEGIANCE
TO THE
GOD
OF MY
UNDERSTANDING,
PARTICIPATING
IN A WORLD
OF GIFTS
AND SURPRISES
NEVER FULLY
EVIDENT
BEFORE
NOW.**

I am embracing
new,
more loving
environments,
people,
and opportunities.

It is all good.

It is
all
Divine.

I am home.

HOW DOES THIS PRAYER APPLY TO YOUR LIFE RIGHT NOW?

WHAT EMOTIONS AND DREAMS DOES THIS BRING UP FOR YOU?

How Would You Modify This Prayer in Your Own Words?

USING THIS PRAYER, WHAT IS ONE STEP YOU CAN DO TO TRANSFORM THE ABUSE YOU'VE ENDURED?

WHO HAVE BEEN
YOUR MOST INSPIRING
TEACHERS IN THIS LIFETIME?
HOW MIGHT THEY RESPOND
TO THIS PRAYER?
WHAT WOULD THEY SHARE
TO SUPPORT YOUR
HEALING PROCESS?

YES,
LORD,
YES TO WHATEVER
IS ASKED
OF
MY DAYS AND
NIGHTS
IN SERVICE
TO
YOU.

YES,
LORD,
YES TO WHAT
IS ASKED
OF
MY DAYS
AND
NIGHTS
IN SERVICE
TO
YOU.

With a new level of faith
I am growing

81

in my quiet conviction
that
**I AM WHERE
I AM SUPPOSED TO BE,
DOING WHAT IS MEANT
FOR ME
TO DO.**

You,
Lord,
have given me reprieve
after reprieve,
no matter
what the circumstances,
forgiven my error actions
and
disappointing behaviors.
It is your forgiveness
of me
which fuels my resolve
to learn
from
my past choices
and
move ahead.

**I AM ARMED
WITH
HARD-WON
LIFE EXPERIENCE.**

I am now choosing,
as never before,
to use that experience
wisely
and
well
as
**ALL I NEED
TO BE
WILDLY SUCCESSFUL
AND EFFECTIVE
IS
WITHIN ME
ALREADY.**

I am so happily blessed.
All is well
with
my soul
today.

Thank You,
God.

Amen.

HOW DOES THIS PRAYER APPLY TO YOUR LIFE RIGHT NOW?

WHAT EMOTIONS AND DREAMS DOES THIS BRING UP FOR YOU?

HOW WOULD YOU MODIFY THIS PRAYER IN YOUR OWN WORDS?

Using This Prayer, What is One Step You Can Do to Transform the Abuse You've Endured?

WHO HAVE BEEN
YOUR MOST INSPIRING
TEACHERS IN THIS LIFETIME?
HOW MIGHT THEY RESPOND
TO THIS PRAYER?
WHAT WOULD THEY SHARE
TO SUPPORT YOUR
HEALING PROCESS?

PRAYER
FOR
ACCEPTING THE
BREAKUP
OF A
LOVE
RELATIONSHIP.

Into any emotional space
where disappointment exists,
hurt reigns like a monarch
drunk with
power.

Hurt and sorrow,
regret and recrimination.

How could I have done it
all better?

More patience?

More romance?

More quality time?

Less pushing?
Less rushing?
More commitment?
Less eagerness?
Less approach-avoidance behavior?

Lord,
I can drive myself
into a ditch of pain
over this situation.

Remind me,
Spirit,
that I am whole,
healthy,
loving and loved
despite the change
of the form
of
love that has occurred.

**I AM MORE
THAN
ANY ONE
RELATIONSHIP.**

**I AM MORE
THAN
ANYONE'S JUDGMENT.**

Each of us possesses
the
inviolable right
to a
change of heart.

WE SHARED WHAT WE SHARED.

THE MEMORIES ARE SACRED.

I cherish what was favorable,
and am open,
receptive and eager
to learn the lessons
of what has transpired.

Inspire in me,
Oh Lord,
the trust in
Your Wisdom

to know this is truly
all in
Divine Order.

How Does This Prayer Apply to Your Life Right Now?

What Emotions and Dreams Does This Bring Up for You?

HOW WOULD YOU MODIFY THIS PRAYER IN YOUR OWN WORDS?

USING THIS PRAYER,
WHAT IS ONE STEP
YOU CAN DO
TO
TRANSFORM THE ABUSE
YOU'VE ENDURED?

WHO HAVE BEEN
YOUR MOST INSPIRING
TEACHERS IN THIS LIFETIME?
HOW MIGHT THEY RESPOND
TO THIS PRAYER?
WHAT WOULD THEY SHARE
TO SUPPORT YOUR
HEALING PROCESS?

UNCERTAINTY ABOUT WHAT IS REAL AND ABSOLUTE.

Oh Lord,

Remind me when
I forget what is real
and absolute
so I live
in the
Light of compassion
and peace.

Inner struggles push
and pull
at my understanding.

Illusion of lack
sometimes seem to replace
Higher Truths
I wish to embrace eternally.

Love is real,
and meant to be kind,
affirming and continual.

Integrity is essential
and designed
to communicate gently
and with
sensitivity.

Protectiveness is absolute
in our efforts
to
shower the inner child
with messages
of
Truth
regarding the birthright
shared by all,
to thrive
in
every way.

Abundance is real.

There is more
than enough
love,
compassion,
bliss,
material
and spiritual
blessings
to go around.

I am willing
to accept all
of this
as
foundational Truth
in my life
here and now.

No one's opinions,
obnoxious insistence
to the contrary,
can interfere
with my healing
and revitalization.

**GOD IN ME
IS INVINCIBLE.**

**I AM
SAFE,
SECURE,
SHOWERED
IN THE
HEALING BALM
OF MY
CONNECTION
TO
GOD.**

May Your Will
be done
in my life,
Amen.

How Does This Prayer Apply to Your Life Right Now?

What Emotions and Dreams Does This Bring Up for You?

How Would You Modify This Prayer in Your Own Words?

USING THIS PRAYER,
WHAT IS ONE STEP
YOU CAN DO
TO
TRANSFORM THE ABUSE
YOU'VE ENDURED?

WHO HAVE BEEN
YOUR MOST INSPIRING
TEACHERS IN THIS LIFETIME?
HOW MIGHT THEY RESPOND
TO THIS PRAYER?
WHAT WOULD THEY SHARE
TO SUPPORT YOUR
HEALING PROCESS?

REJECTION IS ONLY ONE PERSON'S EVALUATION.

Do I perceive
a rejection
in one
area
of my life,
personally
or professionally,
as a rejection
of my
whole being?

Please help me,
Holy Spirit,
to mend those erroneous
imaginings.

Let me remember instead
that each person
has so much more
going on inside their heart,
mind
and circumstances
than I can
ever know.

**WHATEVER THE
CONDITIONS
WHICH MAY HAVE
CAUSED THEM
TO
JUDGE ME,
REJECT
OR
SEVER TIES
WITH ME,
I DO NOT HAVE
THE OMNISCIENCE
TO
KNOW FULLY.**

Let me be comforted
by reminding myself
that I am
Your Beloved Child,
NO MATTER WHAT.

**REJECTION
IS
ONLY
ONE PERSON'S
OPINION.**

Help me appreciate
and be renewed
in the
awareness
of my
good,
caring,
loving
and decent self.

Amen.

How Does This Prayer Apply to Your Life Right Now?

What Emotions and Dreams Does This Bring Up for You?

How Would You Modify This Prayer in Your Own Words?

Using This Prayer, What is One Step You Can Do to Transform the Abuse You've Endured?

WHO HAVE BEEN
YOUR MOST INSPIRING
TEACHERS IN THIS LIFETIME?
HOW MIGHT THEY RESPOND
TO THIS PRAYER?
WHAT WOULD THEY SHARE
TO SUPPORT YOUR
HEALING PROCESS?

Twin Flames/Soul Mate Love.

Beloved Child of Mine,
You have everything needed,
at all times,
to live the loving,
purposeful,
happy
life I envision
for you.

Stand with Me,
hear the guidance,
as I clear away old voices
of self-doubt
and
limited vision,
the
ancient,
ancestral

sufferings
which could keep
holding you back
from the
**UNLIMITED LOVE
YOU ARE.**

Your future
is a
fresh canvas
on which
to paint new images
in
broad,
free
brushstrokes,
bright hues,
original shapes
and
textures.

Love is a blessed foundation
for every
thought,

feeling,
action
and shape
your life takes on.

**WHEN YOUR
INTENTION
IN ALL YOU DO,
AND ARE,
IS TO HONOR
THE DIVINE PRESENCE
24/7,
YOU'VE BECOME
A MASTER ARTIST
IN
LIVING A FULFILLED
LIFE.**

Once this is as natural
as breathing
and exhaling,
you become magnetic
to receiving Good
as never before.

You are engaged
in an
elegant,

organic,
richly loving
process
of honoring your
Divine Nature,
which fosters your ability
to attract
the ideal life partner
when you are both
truly ready.

**GIVE THANKS
IN ADVANCE
OF YOUR
PHYSICAL MEETING
FOR YOUR SOULS
ARE ALREADY
PARTNERING
IN AN
UNBREAKABLE
UNION OF SPIRIT.**

**BE JOYFUL,
FOR THIS LOVE
WILL FIND YOU
AS YOU LET GO
OF THE
FORM,
AND
SAVOR
ALL THE MYRIAD
NUMBER**

**OF
BLESSED WAYS
LOVE HAS,
AND IS,
SHOWING ITS GRACE
IN YOUR LIFE
ALREADY.**

Never doubt
My unending support.

Eternal Blessings,

Your Mother/Father God.

How Does This Prayer Apply to Your Life Right Now?

What Emotions and Dreams Does This Bring Up for You?

How Would You Modify This Prayer in Your Own Words?

USING THIS PRAYER,
WHAT IS ONE STEP
YOU CAN DO
TO
TRANSFORM THE ABUSE
YOU'VE ENDURED?

WHO HAVE BEEN
YOUR MOST INSPIRING
TEACHERS IN THIS LIFETIME?
HOW MIGHT THEY RESPOND
TO THIS PRAYER?
WHAT WOULD THEY SHARE
TO SUPPORT YOUR
HEALING PROCESS?

RELATIONSHIPS
CAN BE
FLEETING.

Relationships,
I've discovered,
Lord,
can be fleeting occurrences.

**MY RELATIONSHIP
WITH YOU
IS BEYOND
DEATH
AND
ORDINARY LIFE.**

There is
only You,
everywhere.

Only Your Love is lasting,
and what infuses us all
with
meaning,
purpose,
true guidance
and
direction.

I am choosing to live this Truth
in my life
and let it inform and direct
all my days and ways.

I am reclaiming the High Road,
and living in renewed,
deepened consciousness
of the sacred process this life allows.

**MY RELATIONSHIP WITH SPIRIT
IS WHAT NOURISHES
THE WELL OF MY RELATIONSHIP
TO MYSELF
AND
EVERYONE ELSE.**

May it be Your Will
that I am able to live at this level
of
intention,
being
and action
indefinitely.

Amen.

How Does This Prayer Apply to Your Life Right Now?

What Emotions and Dreams Does This Bring Up for You?

How Would You Modify This Prayer in Your Own Words?

USING THIS PRAYER,
WHAT IS ONE STEP
YOU CAN DO
TO
TRANSFORM THE ABUSE
YOU'VE ENDURED?

WHO HAVE BEEN
YOUR MOST INSPIRING
TEACHERS IN THIS LIFETIME?
HOW MIGHT THEY RESPOND
TO THIS PRAYER?
WHAT WOULD THEY SHARE
TO SUPPORT YOUR
HEALING PROCESS?

Sweeping Away Negativity.

Narcissistic abuse,
and abuse by other people with
toxic behavioral traits,
has frequently involved
deep,
intractable
negativity.

I have seen,
heard
and been emotionally perplexed
by this.

I am ready for a positive realignment
with the foundation of faith
in the
One Presence and Power everywhere
present to us all.

I cannot control another's choices.

I can control my own by removing myself
from people,
places
and situations
which feel denigrating and dream killing.

I am God's Beloved Child,
heir to all that's good,
beautiful,
and bountiful.

I am claiming and cherishing,
my peace,
contentment
and new direction,
here and now.

LOVE SHOULD NOT BE HURTFUL.

**I AM RECLAIMING MY RIGHT TO LOVE
AND BE LOVED
IN
HEALTHY,
POSITIVE
WAYS
WHICH HONOR
THE
LIGHT OF LIFE.**

I am **THAT**, I am.

Thank You,
God.

So may it be.

HOW DOES THIS PRAYER APPLY TO YOUR LIFE RIGHT NOW?

WHAT EMOTIONS AND DREAMS DOES THIS BRING UP FOR YOU?

HOW WOULD YOU MODIFY THIS PRAYER IN YOUR OWN WORDS?

Using This Prayer, What is One Step You Can Do to Transform the Abuse You've Endured?

WHO HAVE BEEN
YOUR MOST INSPIRING
TEACHERS IN THIS LIFETIME?
HOW MIGHT THEY RESPOND
TO THIS PRAYER?
WHAT WOULD THEY SHARE
TO SUPPORT YOUR
HEALING PROCESS?

Self~Absorption
vs.
Self~ Esteem.

**DEAR LORD,
PLEASE HELP ME REMEMBER
THAT
LOST PEOPLE
OFTEN
LOSE PEOPLE.**

Lost people are experiencing such a level of
unprocessed negative emotions
that there seems to be an
armoring surrounding their hearts.

They are struggling to find a haven
for their hearts.

They can barely respond adequately to
their own needs,
so they glom onto others,
giving just enough of whatever
they perceive the other yearns for,
to ingratiate themselves.

There is no real empathy for the other.

Mostly it is a ploy to form a practical
connection for them to feel
safe,
affirmed,
batteries charged by tremendous
adulation,
affection,
attention...

True self-esteem allows one to know an
inner strength lives,
breathes
and has its origins within
and can offer unlimited self-awareness
and acceptance.

Outside approval,
then,
is **DESIRABLE**.

It **ISN'T NECESSARY**
for peace,
or
a sense of belonging.

People with genuine regard
for their
many virtues

are motivated to keep
growing,
deepening
and becoming ever more able to
share pleasure,
love,
experiences,
and deep communion
with others freely.

They empathize easily.

Thank you,
God,
for showing me the path
which transforms my life to
true embracing
of
Your Divine qualities
in me.

Amen.

.

How Does This Prayer Apply to Your Life Right Now?

What Emotions and Dreams Does This Bring Up for You?

HOW WOULD YOU MODIFY THIS PRAYER IN YOUR OWN WORDS?

USING THIS PRAYER, WHAT IS ONE STEP YOU CAN DO TO TRANSFORM THE ABUSE YOU'VE ENDURED?

WHO HAVE BEEN
YOUR MOST INSPIRING
TEACHERS IN THIS LIFETIME?
HOW MIGHT THEY RESPOND
TO THIS PRAYER?
WHAT WOULD THEY SHARE
TO SUPPORT YOUR
HEALING PROCESS?

TRUST RESTORED, ACCEPTANCE ASSURED.

Oh merciful Lord,
where there is regret,
replace it with acceptance.

Where there is mystification at the
compelling pull of drama
and crazy making,
restore harmony,
encourage peace.

Where there is lust,
imbalanced desire of emotional neediness
and codependent enmeshment,
deliver my heart into your keeping.

**I AM YOUR CHILD,
AND MY TRUST
IS IN THIS PROCESS
OF A RETURN
TO FULL FAITH**

THAT ALL IS IN DIVINE ORDER NOW AND ALWAYS.

Thank You,
Goddess.

Thank You.

Amen.

How Does This Prayer Apply to Your Life Right Now?

What Emotions and Dreams Does This Bring Up for You?

How Would You Modify This Prayer in Your Own Words?

USING THIS PRAYER, WHAT IS ONE STEP YOU CAN DO TO TRANSFORM THE ABUSE YOU'VE ENDURED?

WHO HAVE BEEN
YOUR MOST INSPIRING
TEACHERS IN THIS LIFETIME?
HOW MIGHT THEY RESPOND
TO THIS PRAYER?
WHAT WOULD THEY SHARE
TO SUPPORT YOUR
HEALING PROCESS?

EMOTIONAL RECLAIMING OF INNOCENCE.

I have been injured,
Lord,
by others who act in
unconscious,
careless
manners.
Have I been unconscious,
as well?

**HAVE I BEEN UNTRUE TO MY OWN STANDARDS
IN ORDER TO PLEASE ANOTHER?**

**HAVE I INADVERTENTLY MADE AN IDOL
OF SOMEONE IN THE MISSPOKEN NAME OF
LOVE OR DEVOTION?**

Help me,
Spirit,
to feel your all-encompassing reassurance
all around
and
within me.

How can I find my way clearly back to the
Original Innocence I began with as a baby?

Show me the path You would have me take.

Give me the resolve and the perseverance
to do whatever needs to be achieved.

Provide me,
please,
with the time,
energy
and focus
to remember the solace
which relationship with You
brings.

**I AM YOUR CHILD,
OPEN AS NEVER BEFORE TO
YOUR UNERRING,
GUIDING HAND
OF GENTLENESS
AND STRENGTH.**

My way grows ever smoother.

MY PEACE,
SUCCESS
AND
CONTENTMENT
ARE AT HAND.

Thank You,
God.

Amen.

HOW DOES THIS PRAYER APPLY TO YOUR LIFE RIGHT NOW?

WHAT EMOTIONS AND DREAMS DOES THIS BRING UP FOR YOU?

How Would You Modify This Prayer in Your Own Words?

Using This Prayer, What is One Step You Can Do to Transform the Abuse You've Endured?

WHO HAVE BEEN
YOUR MOST INSPIRING
TEACHERS IN THIS LIFETIME?
HOW MIGHT THEY RESPOND
TO THIS PRAYER?
WHAT WOULD THEY SHARE
TO SUPPORT YOUR
HEALING PROCESS?

CHAPTER 2
EVEN GRIEF CAN BE MOVED THROUGH WITH TENDER MERCIES.

MOURNING
A
RELATIONSHIP.

Changes are an inevitable function
in our lives.

Even though
I am relieved in many ways,
there still is loss
from the ending
of a
relationship.

**I CHOOSE TO EMBRACE
THE MOURNING PROCESS
SO I MAY MOVE BEYOND IT
INTO
THE BRIGHTER LIGHT
OF A NEW DAWN.**

The sun comes up higher
in the sky
of my visions

for a life
more delightful,
a love centered
in the presence
of
God's Infinite Intelligence
and
Devotion.

I am renewed
in the knowing
of my oneness
with the
Divine Essence
that
I AM
always was,
and will be.

How Does This Prayer Apply to Your Life Right Now?

What Emotions and Dreams Does This Bring Up for You?

HOW WOULD YOU MODIFY THIS PRAYER IN YOUR OWN WORDS?

Using This Prayer, What is One Step You Can Do to Transform the Abuse You've Endured?

WHO HAVE BEEN
YOUR MOST INSPIRING
TEACHERS IN THIS LIFETIME?
HOW MIGHT THEY RESPOND
TO THIS PRAYER?
WHAT WOULD THEY SHARE
TO SUPPORT YOUR
HEALING PROCESS?

GRIEVING POINTS ME IN A HAPPIER DIRECTION NOW.

Abuse survivors inevitably
endure the process
of grieving
what has happened.

Though
the
discomfort,
sorrow,
and
bitter sweetness
doesn't have to last forever,
there may be moments
when it feels
like an unending curse.
It isn't.

Grieving
points me

in a
happier direction
now.

I have been shown how painful
what was,
actually **WAS**.

Through this insight
I am learning
what to avoid
in the
present
and
future.

Grieving also alerts me
to what was once beneficial
which has had to
change form.

I am willing to
see,
know
and
face
all of it,
the good,
bad,
beautiful

161

and ugly
memories
and
emotions.

**I LOOK
TO THE
DIVINE PRESENCE
WITHIN AND ALL AROUND
TO REPLENISH
MY RESOLVE
AND TO
REKINDLE
MY BUOYANCY.**

**I AM RESILIENT
AND
I AM CHOOSING
TO BOUNCE
BACK.**

I count up my losses
and see them as necessary
to create the vacuum
for better
relationships,
opportunities
and
strong faith
to come.

The blessings are abounding.

In Gratitude.

HOW DOES THIS PRAYER APPLY TO YOUR LIFE RIGHT NOW?

WHAT EMOTIONS AND DREAMS DOES THIS BRING UP FOR YOU?

HOW WOULD YOU MODIFY THIS PRAYER IN YOUR OWN WORDS?

Using This Prayer, What is One Step You Can Do to Transform the Abuse You've Endured?

WHO HAVE BEEN
YOUR MOST INSPIRING
TEACHERS IN THIS LIFETIME?
HOW MIGHT THEY RESPOND
TO THIS PRAYER?
WHAT WOULD THEY SHARE
TO SUPPORT YOUR
HEALING PROCESS?

Even Grief
Can Be Moved
Through
with
Tender Mercies,
Grace Unlimited,
When I Call
on
My Faith.

So many of us have distracted ourselves
from feeling our grief over
loss,
abuse,
shattered plans
and
fractured dreams.

Maybe we were so unaware
we never saw it coming.

Possibly we saw it coming
and were too terrified
of the
unknown to leave.

THE PAST IS OVER.

THE PRESENT IS HERE NOW.

**I AM READY AND EAGER
TO FEEL
FULLY
AGAIN.**

Even grief can be moved
through with
tender mercies,
grace unlimited,
when I call
on my
faith.

I am willing to feel this
sadness
and
embrace
new possibilities

169

for my
highest benefit,
and the good
of others
as well.

Thank you,
Spirit,
for enfolding my life
in Love.

I am grateful.

I am **THAT** I am.

I am **THAT**,
I truly am.

Amen.

.

How Does This Prayer Apply to Your Life Right Now?

What Emotions and Dreams Does This Bring Up for You?

How Would You Modify This Prayer in Your Own Words?

USING THIS PRAYER, WHAT IS ONE STEP YOU CAN DO TO TRANSFORM THE ABUSE YOU'VE ENDURED?

WHO HAVE BEEN
YOUR MOST INSPIRING
TEACHERS IN THIS LIFETIME?
HOW MIGHT THEY RESPOND
TO THIS PRAYER?
WHAT WOULD THEY SHARE
TO SUPPORT YOUR
HEALING PROCESS?

GRIEF
IS A GIFT,
LIKE EVERY OTHER
EMOTION,
TO
ALERT
MY AWARENESS.

Dear God,

Grief can feel like a dull ache,
or,
a smoldering ember
from a fire
which refuses
to go out.

**GIVE ME RELIEF,
LOVING AND COMPASSIONATE
SPIRIT,
FROM WHAT SEEMS
UNJUST,
WHAT FEELS LIKE
A MAELSTROM
OF EMOTIONS...**

**WHAT CONTINUALLY DISTRACTS ME
FROM SEEING THE JOY POSSIBLE
TO EXPERIENCE AND SHARE.**

Though it may be hard to remember
at times,
I am capable of staying fully present
wherever I am,
whatever I do.

In this moment,
I can breathe in
solace,
harmony,
comfort...

In this day
I am able to find a blessing
right here,
right now.

**GRIEF
IS A GIFT,
LIKE EVERY OTHER
EMOTION,
TO
ALERT
MY AWARENESS.**

It is a barometer
of whatever I'm choosing
to think right now.

FEELINGS CHANGE.

EMOTIONS ARE TEMPORARY.

Whatever,
or,
whomever has been lost,
**I HAVE THE POWER TO CHOOSE ANOTHER
THOUGHT
WHICH ALLOWS
FOR THE NATURAL PROGRESSION
TO A
HIGHER LEVEL
OF UNDERSTANDING,
A LIGHTER MOOD.**

**HELP ME ALLOW MYSELF
TO FEEL EACH WAVE OF EMOTION
AS IT FLOWS WITHOUT FEAR
OR
RESISTANCE.**

Give me rest,
Precious Spirit,
so I can free my mind
and heart to be fully empowered
in living
a vitally alive

and vibrant
life,
as
never before.

How Does This Prayer Apply to Your Life Right Now?

What Emotions and Dreams Does This Bring Up for You?

How Would You Modify This Prayer in Your Own Words?

Using This Prayer, What is One Step You Can Do to Transform the Abuse You've Endured?

WHO HAVE BEEN
YOUR MOST INSPIRING
TEACHERS IN THIS LIFETIME?
HOW MIGHT THEY RESPOND
TO THIS PRAYER?
WHAT WOULD THEY SHARE
TO SUPPORT YOUR
HEALING PROCESS?

BEFORE I EVER CALL, YOUR LOVE WARMS, SURROUNDS AND ENFOLDS ME IN PROTECTIVE LIGHT.

Even if grief has tried to set up
housekeeping in my mind
and heart,
Divine Presence,
it's becoming clear to me
that BEFORE I EVER CALL,
YOUR LOVE
WARMS,
SURROUNDS
AND
ENFOLDS ME
IN
PROTECTIVE LIGHT.

183

GIVE ME
THE SPIRITUAL EYES
TO SEE
THIS PHENOMENON
MORE READILY.

PROVIDE FOR ME
THE SPIRITUAL EARS
TO HEAR
THE UNIQUE LANGUAGE
YOU USE TO SPEAK
TO MY SENSIBILITY.

I AM YOUR BELOVED CHILD,
HEIR TO EVERY GOOD
IMAGINABLE.

Whatever loss
or sadness
has caused grief to visit my
life,
I AM WILLING TO EXPERIENCE
THE FEELINGS.

TRUSTING THAT THESE HEAVY
SADNESSES,
REGRETS,
FEELINGS
OF
OPPORTUNITIES LOST,

**OR SOMEONE MISSING,
ARE SIMPLY
A NECESSARY PROCESSING
OF
UNDIGESTED EMOTIONS,
I AM UNAFRAID.**

You are with me,
now,
and
always.

I am in service to
Your Light.

Amen.

How Does This Prayer Apply to Your Life Right Now?

What Emotions and Dreams Does This Bring Up for You?

How Would You Modify This Prayer in Your Own Words?

USING THIS PRAYER, WHAT IS ONE STEP YOU CAN DO TO TRANSFORM THE ABUSE YOU'VE ENDURED?

WHO HAVE BEEN
YOUR MOST INSPIRING
TEACHERS IN THIS LIFETIME?
HOW MIGHT THEY RESPOND
TO THIS PRAYER?
WHAT WOULD THEY SHARE
TO SUPPORT YOUR
HEALING PROCESS?

CONSCIENCE CLEANSED
OF
UNWARRANTED
GUILT.

Even when misguided guilt
strives to set up housekeeping
in my mind,
I know that You,
Holy Spirit,
within me is working miracles.

Keep those miraculous shifts
coming into my being.

A conscience
is a
beautiful
Inner Guidance System
leading us
in a
favorable direction.

It can,
however,
sometimes
become a mechanism
for torture,
and turmoil
at times.

When I can allow myself
to trust that all **IS** occurring
and everything **DID** occur,
in Divine Order,
my peace transcends
sorrow,
defeat,
fatigue,
feeling like a beaten up prize fighter
profoundly bruised
by life.

Keep working
cleansing changes
to free me
from within.

Thank You,
Lord.

**I REST
IN THE
INFINITE ASSURANCE
OF
YOUR SHELTERING
PROTECTION.**

How Does This Prayer Apply to Your Life Right Now?

What Emotions and Dreams Does This Bring Up for You?

How Would You Modify This Prayer in Your Own Words?

USING THIS PRAYER, WHAT IS ONE STEP YOU CAN DO TO TRANSFORM THE ABUSE YOU'VE ENDURED?

WHO HAVE BEEN
YOUR MOST INSPIRING
TEACHERS IN THIS LIFETIME?
HOW MIGHT THEY RESPOND
TO THIS PRAYER?
WHAT WOULD THEY SHARE
TO SUPPORT YOUR
HEALING PROCESS?

HEALING
IS
A CONTINUING
PROCESS
OF
LETTING GO
OF
HAVING
TO BE
RIGHT.

Release me,
Lord,
from all binding beliefs
of the past
borne of fear.
Those ideas,
beliefs
and values
are the precursors
of the
idea

197

that
**I HAVE
TO BE RIGHT
ALL THE TIME.**

They doom me
to obstinacy.

They condemn me
to harsh positions
which can feel
unshakable.

**I DESIRE A NEW IDEA
TO
FREE ME.**

I've observed
these destructive patterns
of behavior
in others,
and now
am realizing
they may have reflected
some part
of this
in me.

Help me be more patient
with others.

198

HELP ME,
PLEASE,
TO REMEMBER
THAT HEALING
IS A
CONTINUING PROCESS
OF
LETTING GO
OF
HAVING
TO BE RIGHT.

In the overall scheme
of things,
will I even remember
what seemed
so crucial
to insist on
in a month
or
in a year?

Thank You,
God,
for
answered prayers.

Amen.

How Does This Prayer Apply to Your Life Right Now?

What Emotions and Dreams Does This Bring Up for You?

HOW WOULD YOU MODIFY
THIS PRAYER IN YOUR
OWN WORDS?

USING THIS PRAYER, WHAT IS ONE STEP YOU CAN DO TO TRANSFORM THE ABUSE YOU'VE ENDURED?

WHO HAVE BEEN
YOUR MOST INSPIRING
TEACHERS IN THIS LIFETIME?
HOW MIGHT THEY RESPOND
TO THIS PRAYER?
WHAT WOULD THEY SHARE
TO SUPPORT YOUR
HEALING PROCESS?

CHAPTER 3
FORGIVENESS.

Prayer to Heal Regret; Work a Miracle in Me, Holy Spirit.

Love is designed to uplift
and make us more of who we truly are,
yet I trusted someone who mangled
my caring,
and discarded the gift of devotion offered.

WORK A MIRACLE IN ME,
HOLY SPIRIT.

I missed the mark by attracting,
and remaining with a relationship
which was far from the
stability,
honesty,
harmony,
communication,
faithfulness,
and compassion
I know we all deserve.

If to sin means to miss the mark,
I've sinned.

Help me choose again,
Lord.

**FIRST,
HELP ME FORGIVE MYSELF
AND HAVE RENEWED INSIGHT INTO
WHAT GIFTS THIS PERSON CAME
TO BRING ME
FOR
MY GROWTH.**

I am willing to see,
hear,
and embrace the truth
so I can move on to more
joy,
freedom,
expanded consciousness,
and healthy love.

It is a process of seeing what error thoughts
created the vulnerability
**OF
IGNORING EARLY SIGNS
OF A TWO-FACED PERSON,
EARLY INDICATORS
OF**

**INSINCERITY,
AND LACK OF EMPATHY.**

I deserve better from myself and others.

**IT ALL CENTERS ON MY RELATIONSHIP
WITH YOUR LOVE,
SO I AM SAFELY HELD
IN AN EVERLASTING EMBRACE
OF THE
DIVINE.**

Thank You!

How Does This Prayer Apply to Your Life Right Now?

What Emotions and Dreams Does This Bring Up for You?

How Would You Modify This Prayer in Your Own Words?

USING THIS PRAYER,
WHAT IS ONE STEP
YOU CAN DO
TO
TRANSFORM THE ABUSE
YOU'VE ENDURED?

WHO HAVE BEEN
YOUR MOST INSPIRING
TEACHERS IN THIS LIFETIME?
HOW MIGHT THEY RESPOND
TO THIS PRAYER?
WHAT WOULD THEY SHARE
TO SUPPORT YOUR
HEALING PROCESS?

FORGIVING
THE
SEEMINGLY
UNFORGIVABLE.

Reconnect me,
Lord,
to that place of compassion
which loves the You in me enough
to forgive what is seemingly unforgivable.

With Your Love, I can do this.

**WITH YOUR INFINITE SUPPORT
I CAN CHOOSE A SMOOTHER ROAD,
A HIGHER PATH DEVOID OF
GRIEVANCES,
REGRETS,
LOST DREAMS
AND BITTERNESS.**

I am choosing to pray for the
happiness of everyone,
no matter who they are
or
what they've done,
or,
failed to do.

**I AM LEARNING TO LOVE MYSELF
ENOUGH
TO REJECT
ANY THOUGHTS
THAT PROMOTE
TOXIC EMOTIONS.**

I have a new chance to live life
as an informed being
of radiant light.

I am living in that spirit
and dancing
out of darkness.

Thank You, Thank You,
God.

Amen.

How Does This Prayer
Apply to Your Life
Right Now?

What Emotions
and Dreams Does
This Bring Up for
You?

HOW WOULD YOU MODIFY
THIS PRAYER IN YOUR
OWN WORDS?

USING THIS PRAYER, WHAT IS ONE STEP YOU CAN DO TO TRANSFORM THE ABUSE YOU'VE ENDURED?

WHO HAVE BEEN
YOUR MOST INSPIRING
TEACHERS IN THIS LIFETIME?
HOW MIGHT THEY RESPOND
TO THIS PRAYER?
WHAT WOULD THEY SHARE
TO SUPPORT YOUR
HEALING PROCESS?

GOD FORGIVES US BEFORE WE EVEN FORGIVE OURSELVES OR OTHERS.

I am deeply moved
by the realization
of the
Truth of God's forgiveness.

GOD FORGIVES US BEFORE WE EVEN FORGIVE OURSELVES OR OTHERS.

Benevolence,
forgiveness,
integrity,
reliability,
compassion,
unconditional acceptance
are all Divine Qualities
hard-wired into our DNA
by the
Divine Designer of All There Is or ever was.

218

**BECAUSE GOD FORGIVES,
I CAN STOP REJECTING AND CONDEMNING
MYSELF.**

**BECAUSE GOD FORGIVES,
I CAN STOP REJECTING AND CONDEMNING
OTHERS.**

Condemnation arises from fear.

Unconditional caring arises from love.

**GOD IS THE LOVE I HAVE ALWAYS YEARNED
FOR,**
and has been in,
through,
and as me,
as all of us,
all along,
despite personality driven behaviors
sometimes showing up as
less than divine.

Thank You, Divine Presence,
for Your unerring power
to restore my strength,

deepen my faith
and my decision
to stop harsh pronouncements
of
myself and others.

Amen.

How Does This Prayer Apply to Your Life Right Now?

What Emotions and Dreams Does This Bring Up for You?

How Would You Modify This Prayer in Your Own Words?

USING THIS PRAYER, WHAT IS ONE STEP YOU CAN DO TO TRANSFORM THE ABUSE YOU'VE ENDURED?

WHO HAVE BEEN
YOUR MOST INSPIRING
TEACHERS IN THIS LIFETIME?
HOW MIGHT THEY RESPOND
TO THIS PRAYER?
WHAT WOULD THEY SHARE
TO SUPPORT YOUR
HEALING PROCESS?

TREASURES ARE AMPLIFIED WHEN SHARED.

Like a healing dove,
mercy flows into each area of my life.

I am richly blessed.

I am gratitude- filled.

I am determined as never before,
to share my gifts,
talents and aptitudes
with others in forms
acceptable to them.

TREASURES ARE AMPLIFIED WHEN SHARED.

I am a sharer of the unlimited good now in
whatever ways are for the best
and highest of all.

This level of clarity relieves doubts,
redoubles my strength
and delivers optimism to my heart,
mind and body.

Surely with awareness of such
powerful blessings,
I can choose to release harmlessly
whatever pain of the past may
have obstructed **MY SMOOTH PATH**
up to now.

I am blessed and a blessing.

May it be Thy Will

Amen.

HOW DOES THIS PRAYER APPLY TO YOUR LIFE RIGHT NOW?

WHAT EMOTIONS AND DREAMS DOES THIS BRING UP FOR YOU?

How Would You Modify This Prayer in Your Own Words?

Using This Prayer, What is One Step You Can Do to Transform the Abuse You've Endured?

WHO HAVE BEEN
YOUR MOST INSPIRING
TEACHERS IN THIS LIFETIME?
HOW MIGHT THEY RESPOND
TO THIS PRAYER?
WHAT WOULD THEY SHARE
TO SUPPORT YOUR
HEALING PROCESS?

EMBARRASSMENT
CAN LEAD
TO
RESENTMENT.

At no time do we ever enjoy feeling like we
aren't completely understood,
accepted
and honored
by those around us.

Overly critical people,
whether family,
friends,
co-workers
or strangers
can create resentment
if they treat us harshly.

**EMBARRASSMENT CAN LEAD TO FEELINGS
OF RESENTMENT.**

REMIND ME,
LORD,
NOT TO TAKE ANYTHING SO PERSONALLY
ANYMORE.

NOT ONLY DO
NASTINESS,
DISRESPECT
AND REJECTION
REFLECT MUCH MORE ON THE INDIVIDUAL
WHO IS PERPETRATING THE NEGATIVITY,
IT OFTEN HAS VERY LITTLE TO DO WITH
ME,
OR,
WHOMEVER IT'S AIMED AT.
AS YOUR BELOVED CHILD,
I CAN REMAIN CENTERED
IN AN INNER CALMNESS
WHICH OVERRIDES
OUTER DISAPPROVAL.

I am more than enough of all that is
favorable,
valuable
and capable.

I AM EQUAL TO
WHATEVER TASK IS BEFORE ME,
SO,

**RELEASING RESENTMENT
IS NOW TRANSFORMED
INTO A
SEAMLESS PROCESS.**

I **CHOOSE** to let go,
turning the actions,
both happy,
sad,
kind,
or,
mean,
over to Your care and keeping,
Gracious and Loving Spirit.

What a relief it is
to let the feelings
which were binding me to exactly what I
need freedom from,
simply go back to the nothingness
from whence they arose.

Thank You,
Loving Spirit.

How Does This Prayer Apply to Your Life Right Now?

What Emotions and Dreams Does This Bring Up for You?

How Would You Modify This Prayer in Your Own Words?

USING THIS PRAYER,
WHAT IS ONE STEP
YOU CAN DO
TO
TRANSFORM THE ABUSE
YOU'VE ENDURED?

WHO HAVE BEEN
YOUR MOST INSPIRING
TEACHERS IN THIS LIFETIME?
HOW MIGHT THEY RESPOND
TO THIS PRAYER?
WHAT WOULD THEY SHARE
TO SUPPORT YOUR
HEALING PROCESS?

CHAPTER 4
SURVIVING THE FALLOUT FROM ABUSE, THE BLESSINGS DISCERNED.

Aftermath
of
Narcissistic
Abuse
Survivorship.

Deliver me from unresolved dreams
and sorrowful,
poignant events,
please,
Lord.

Narcissistic abuse can leave even a
once self-confident person
in an emotional mine field of doubt,
despair
and confusion.

**I AM MEETING MY FEELINGS
WITH
ENTHUSIASM
BECAUSE I HAVE SURVIVED
THE
WORST.**

In faith
I can embrace far more mutually
caring,

239

compassionate,
supportive possibilities.

Better situations,
times and people are being drawn
into my life.

Renewal and reverification
of my
reclaimed inherent grace,
intelligence,
self-assurance
and dignity are stronger
by the day.

No one can disturb this harmony
because it is of the
Divine Nature
from whence I came.

**GIVE ME THE FORBEARANCE TO
RELEASE
OLD PAIN AND KEEP UPLIFTING
MY THOUGHT PROCESS
SO I MAY BE WHO
I CAME HERE TO BE,
AND LIVE THE LIFE
I AM DESTINED
TO BE
BLESSED WITH.**

I am not bitter,
I am better.

I am not downtrodden.

I am receiving new insights as I ask and
Divine Love responds in
beneficial,
comforting ways.

Thank You,
and
amen.

How Does This Prayer Apply to Your Life Right Now?

What Emotions and Dreams Does This Bring Up for You?

How Would You Modify This Prayer in Your Own Words?

Using This Prayer, What is One Step You Can Do to Transform the Abuse You've Endured?

WHO HAVE BEEN
YOUR MOST INSPIRING
TEACHERS IN THIS LIFETIME?
HOW MIGHT THEY RESPOND
TO THIS PRAYER?
WHAT WOULD THEY SHARE
TO SUPPORT YOUR
HEALING PROCESS?

DISAPPOINTMENT
WILL NOT
DEFEAT ME.

How do I deal with disappointment,
Holy Spirit?

How do I piece together
broken hopes and dreams
to see the light of gift and blessing
contained within the situation?

How do I remember to release the
hurt,
discouragement,
distrust
and doubt
to dance into the Light
of a new way
to approach love?

When is it my turn to turn away from the
wasp's sting of sorrow and alienation?

Anger is just a smokescreen for fear of
inadequacy,
a stand-in for doubts
about ever having what I say I want
most.

GET ME TO THE CORE ISSUES,
HOLY SPIRIT,
with as much tender
mercy,
grace
and integrity
as possible.

I AM SO WILLING.

FEAR IS NO OPPONENT
FOR THE
LOVE YOU ARE,
AND
I AM,
TOO.

HOW DOES THIS PRAYER APPLY TO YOUR LIFE RIGHT NOW?

WHAT EMOTIONS AND DREAMS DOES THIS BRING UP FOR YOU?

How Would You Modify This Prayer in Your Own Words?

USING THIS PRAYER, WHAT IS ONE STEP YOU CAN DO TO TRANSFORM THE ABUSE YOU'VE ENDURED?

WHO HAVE BEEN
YOUR MOST INSPIRING
TEACHERS IN THIS LIFETIME?
HOW MIGHT THEY RESPOND
TO THIS PRAYER?
WHAT WOULD THEY SHARE
TO SUPPORT YOUR
HEALING PROCESS?

LOVING UNCONDITIONALLY FROM A SAFE DISTANCE.

Keep working miracles of new
awareness here,
Holy Spirit.

I am loving by my very nature.

I am born to love and be loved as the
Divine Presence
loves me.

Loving unconditionally
**DOES NOT MEAN
ACCEPTING ABUSE.**

Loving unconditionally does not mean
sacrificing my hope of a
healthy,
mutually caring,
stable,
enduring
relationship.

**HELP ME,
LORD,
TO DISCERN WHEN
TO LOVE
UNCONDITIONALLY
BY HOLDING SOMEONE
IN THE
LIGHT OF PRAYER,
FROM A SAFE DISTANCE.**

Remind me gently,
Holy Spirit,
that **MY PEACE MUST BE THE PRIORITY.**
My safety,
health,
well-being
must never be given away
in the name of love.

My well will always be refilled
with my faith.

How Does This Prayer Apply to Your Life Right Now?

What Emotions and Dreams Does This Bring Up for You?

How Would You Modify This Prayer in Your Own Words?

USING THIS PRAYER, WHAT IS ONE STEP YOU CAN DO TO TRANSFORM THE ABUSE YOU'VE ENDURED?

WHO HAVE BEEN
YOUR MOST INSPIRING
TEACHERS IN THIS LIFETIME?
HOW MIGHT THEY RESPOND
TO THIS PRAYER?
WHAT WOULD THEY SHARE
TO SUPPORT YOUR
HEALING PROCESS?

EVERYONE
IS A
SURVIVOR
OF
SOMETHING!

Everyone is a survivor of something!

Whether it's
rape,
incest,
substance abuse,
bankruptcy,
illness,
being fired,
laid off,
having been held back in school a grade,
rejection,
depression,
debt,
gambling,
co-dependency,

narcissistic abuse,
separation,
divorce,
loss of loved ones
to life changes,
to physical death, etc....

Everyone's journey is the soul's path
needed for their evolution
in this lifetime.

**MANY ARE SIMILAR,
YET NO TWO PATHS ARE IDENTICAL
BECAUSE EACH SOUL
IS UNIQUE.**

In the past
I may not have recognized my own,
or others', individual curriculum
in this
Earthly School of Spiritual Unfoldment.

I am recognizing it now.

Thank You, God.

I am changed for the better.

May my life be an ever-better channel
for blessing others.

Amen.

How Does This Prayer Apply to Your Life Right Now?

What Emotions and Dreams Does This Bring Up for You?

How Would You Modify This Prayer in Your Own Words?

Using This Prayer, What is One Step You Can Do to Transform the Abuse You've Endured?

WHO HAVE BEEN
YOUR MOST INSPIRING
TEACHERS IN THIS LIFETIME?
HOW MIGHT THEY RESPOND
TO THIS PRAYER?
WHAT WOULD THEY SHARE
TO SUPPORT YOUR
HEALING PROCESS?

BELEAGUERED
NO MORE.

I have felt the oppression
of unresolved desires
in a
dead-end relationship
doomed from the start.
Discouragement caused by another's
unpredictability,
broken promises,
shifting moods,
lies
and more distortions,
has left me feeling exhausted.

I acknowledge all the feelings.

Life was never meant to be
total ecstasy
all the time.

Lessons and gifts do not always arrive in
silver slippers
and cut crystal champagne goblets.

I know.

I am ready,
however,
to see the aspects
of
what has occurred,
or
still is happening,
with open receptivity
to the
Truth.

What is it in my core beliefs which
need to be adjusted?

How do I celebrate what was
and is good,
and move ahead in a most
graceful,
blessed
manner?

I give thanks for
answers arriving
in wondrous ways.

I NOW DIRECT MY VOICE,
MY THOUGHTS,
MY MOVEMENTS,
MY ACTIONS
TO BE TOTALLY IN TANDEM
WITH
DIVINE LOVE.

Nothing less is acceptable
from this moment forward.

No excuses,
no lapses,
no looking outside myself for affirmation,
just corroboration
of what I already embrace
as my Higher Life Vision.

God is in charge of my ways as never before.

I AM UPLIFTED AND AM NOW ENGAGED
IN A NEW LEVEL OF ABILITY
TO BE A GIFT AND BLESSING
TO OTHERS AROUND ME.

I am so richly inspired
and reassured as
God speaks through me daily.

I listen carefully
recognizing that all
gratefulness,
and praise,
goes to the
One.

Amen.

How Does This Prayer Apply to Your Life Right Now?

What Emotions and Dreams Does This Bring Up for You?

How Would You Modify This Prayer in Your Own Words?

USING THIS PRAYER, WHAT IS ONE STEP YOU CAN DO TO TRANSFORM THE ABUSE YOU'VE ENDURED?

WHO HAVE BEEN
YOUR MOST INSPIRING
TEACHERS IN THIS LIFETIME?
HOW MIGHT THEY RESPOND
TO THIS PRAYER?
WHAT WOULD THEY SHARE
TO SUPPORT YOUR
HEALING PROCESS?

HEALING
FROM
BETRAYAL.

My trust has been shaken,
Holy Spirit.

How can I ever risk trusting fully again
when someone could destroy credibility
again and again?

Show me a new road,
light-filled
and safe,
unshackled by dishonesty and cruelty.

There must be a place of gentler communion
than what has transpired.

**IF FEAR GRIPS ME LIKE A TIGHT,
ROUGH VISE,
I WILL CHALLENGE IT
WITH MY KNOWING THAT MY VALUE,
DESIRES,**

**DREAMS
AND GOALS
ARISE FROM THE UNLIMITED
GOOD
GOD IS.**

**NO
PERSON,
PLACE
OR SITUATION
IS MY SUPPLY.**

My Source is the Divine,
therefore I am
safe,
secure
and filled
with the
Light of uplifting thoughts and ideas.

No one can change this Truth.

Peace,
therefore,
is mine.

RENEWAL IS MINE.

**TRANQUILITY
IS MY
NATURAL STATE.**

I name it
and claim it
here and now.

Thank You,
Lord.

Amen.

How Does This Prayer Apply to Your Life Right Now?

What Emotions and Dreams Does This Bring Up for You?

HOW WOULD YOU MODIFY THIS PRAYER IN YOUR OWN WORDS?

USING THIS PRAYER,
WHAT IS ONE STEP
YOU CAN DO
TO
TRANSFORM THE ABUSE
YOU'VE ENDURED?

WHO HAVE BEEN
YOUR MOST INSPIRING
TEACHERS IN THIS LIFETIME?
HOW MIGHT THEY RESPOND
TO THIS PRAYER?
WHAT WOULD THEY SHARE
TO SUPPORT YOUR
HEALING PROCESS?

I Am
Grace,
Compassion,
Integrity
and Wisdom
in Action.

A narcissistic relationship
can villify all that feels loving,
life-enhancing
and joy-reinforcing
as it goes along,
so can it be a blessed chance
to **LEARN DISCERNMENT**.

Though my trust has been rocked
like an emotional earthquake,
a resilient part of the heart
remembers that a far better time
is ahead.

Restore my ability to discern when,
and how,
to safeguard immediately
should I ever attract anyone
with these complexities again.

I am Your Child.

Being cradled in your
ever-present arms,
all doubts are erased.

The interconnectedness
with
Divine Love
brings reclaimed harmony.

**THRIVING IS NOW NOT
ONLY
POSSIBLE.**

IT IS BECOMING MY REALITY,

With God,
truly happiness is mine.

Peace is mine.

RECONNECTION
TO A
JOYFUL PROCESS
IS MINE

MY DIVINE INHERITANCE IS RECEIVED.

I am blessed,
and a blessing.
I am grace,
compassion,
integrity
and wisdom
in action.

I am **THAT**,
I am

Amen
and
Thank You,
Lord.

How Does This Prayer Apply to Your Life Right Now?

What Emotions and Dreams Does This Bring Up for You?

How Would You Modify This Prayer in Your Own Words?

USING THIS PRAYER, WHAT IS ONE STEP YOU CAN DO TO TRANSFORM THE ABUSE YOU'VE ENDURED?

WHO HAVE BEEN
YOUR MOST INSPIRING
TEACHERS IN THIS LIFETIME?
HOW MIGHT THEY RESPOND
TO THIS PRAYER?
WHAT WOULD THEY SHARE
TO SUPPORT YOUR
HEALING PROCESS?

CHAPTER 5

OVERCOMING DISCOURAGEMENT AND RECONNECTING TO JOY.

INTERRUPTING THE ENERGY OF LETHARGY AND APATHY.

After,

or,

during a toxic episode,
lethargy and apathy
can insidiously enter.

Unwelcome,
uninvited visitors,
they are borne of
discouragement,
disillusionment
and old,
destructive beliefs.

Lethargy and apathy
are also results
of

exhaustion,
feeling emotionally handicapped
from
profound grief
and inconsistent treatment.

Oh,
Lord,
remind me of the awesome,
enlivened potency
of
Your Spark
living within my hopeful heart.

I am resilient,
willing to participate in rejuvenation.

**I AM SO GRATEFUL TO BE RENEWED
BY THE
SPIRIT OF ABSOLUTE GOOD:
PHYSICALLY
INTELLECTUALLY
EMOTIONALLY
SPIRITUALLY
FINANCIALLY**

**PERSONALLY
AND
PROFESSIONALLY
NOW.**

May it be Your Will.

Amen.

.

HOW DOES THIS PRAYER APPLY TO YOUR LIFE RIGHT NOW?

WHAT EMOTIONS AND DREAMS DOES THIS BRING UP FOR YOU?

How Would You Modify This Prayer in Your Own Words?

Using This Prayer, What is One Step You Can Do to Transform the Abuse You've Endured?

WHO HAVE BEEN
YOUR MOST INSPIRING
TEACHERS IN THIS LIFETIME?
HOW MIGHT THEY RESPOND
TO THIS PRAYER?
WHAT WOULD THEY SHARE
TO SUPPORT YOUR
HEALING PROCESS?

A
THRIVING EXISTENCE
NOW.

My life is a Divine Idea
in the Heart of God
which has come to earth
for unique experiences
and
purposes.

.

I am now living in the loving,
and caring awareness of this Truth
governing my wellness
physically,
emotionally,
mentally,
spiritually,
and vocationally.

This awareness creates a Divine Shield
protecting me from any harsh thought
forms within,
or,
around me
in the environment.

I am only available to give and receive
compassion,
kindness,
playfulness,
exploration,
adventures,
and co-creative ventures
with like-hearted people.

**I AM DRAWING TO ME
ALL THE RIGHT CONDITIONS
FOR A
RENEWED
AND
THRIVING EXISTENCE
NOW.**

Such thanks is given for
gifts,
wonders
and serendipitous surprises
when I least expect them.
Thank You,
Thank You,
Thank You...
amen.

HOW DOES THIS PRAYER APPLY TO YOUR LIFE RIGHT NOW?

WHAT EMOTIONS AND DREAMS DOES THIS BRING UP FOR YOU?

How Would You Modify This Prayer in Your Own Words?

Using This Prayer,
What is One Step
You Can Do
to
Transform the Abuse
You've Endured?

Who Have Been Your Most Inspiring Teachers in This Lifetime? How Might They Respond to This Prayer? What Would They Share to Support Your Healing Process?

STRONGER AT THE BROKEN PLACES.

Why might I find it easier
to nurture others
than to be generous to myself?

Aren't I a human being,
therefore,
deserving of the same
unconditional acceptance
showered on all of your Children,
Lord?

Has something in my thought process
been compromised by my earlier life?

By current situations and tragedies?

I am willing to be stronger
at the broken places
in my faithfulness
to my faith.

My faith fully embraces the Divine within
as my Rock and Reassurance
that all is unfolding well.

Nothing is lacking in my life.

There is more than enough of all
that is
life-affirming and constructive.

**THE FULLNESS OF BLESSINGS
ARE NOW MY PRIMARY FOCUS,
SO I AM EXPERIENCING MORE GRACE
AND GRATITUDE THAN EVER BEFORE.**

What blessings are revealed
moment to moment.

**I AM STRONG,
WHOLE,
PURPOSEFUL
AND
FREE.**

I am **THAT**,
I am.

I am **THAT**,
I truly am.

Thank You,
Spirit,
for the process of life
which uplifts,
transcends
and illuminates
every old shadow.

Amen.

HOW DOES THIS PRAYER APPLY TO YOUR LIFE RIGHT NOW?

WHAT EMOTIONS AND DREAMS DOES THIS BRING UP FOR YOU?

How Would You Modify This Prayer in Your Own Words?

USING THIS PRAYER, WHAT IS ONE STEP YOU CAN DO TO TRANSFORM THE ABUSE YOU'VE ENDURED?

WHO HAVE BEEN
YOUR MOST INSPIRING
TEACHERS IN THIS LIFETIME?
HOW MIGHT THEY RESPOND
TO THIS PRAYER?
WHAT WOULD THEY SHARE
TO SUPPORT YOUR
HEALING PROCESS?

RECONNECTING
TO
MY AWARENESS
OF
SELF~WORTH.

Divine Presence,
Thank You for reconnecting me
to my awareness
of
self-worth.

**I AM YOUR BELOVED CHILD,
NO MATTER WHERE I'VE BEEN,
NO MATTER WHAT INDIGNITIES
HAVE BEEN ENDURED.**

Your love for me transcends
all human earthly experiences.

Knowing this, I am willing to consider
reclaiming my fullness,
wellness,
and living

from a renewed sense of
life's unlimited potential for good.

**NO MATTER HOW DIRE MY TREATMENT
MAY HAVE BEEN,
OR STILL MAY BE,
I AM MORE THAN THIS STORY.**

I am more than the
lack,
limitation,
dream crushing,
self-esteem bashing injustices,
this world can ever touch.

I am so grateful to be revitalized
by this
unchanging Truth
about myself,
and others.

My healing accelerates accordingly now.

Thank You,
Thank You,
Thank You,
Divine Essence.

How Does This Prayer Apply to Your Life Right Now?

What Emotions and Dreams Does This Bring Up for You?

How Would You Modify This Prayer in Your Own Words?

USING THIS PRAYER,
WHAT IS ONE STEP
YOU CAN DO
TO
TRANSFORM THE ABUSE
YOU'VE ENDURED?

WHO HAVE BEEN
YOUR MOST INSPIRING
TEACHERS IN THIS LIFETIME?
HOW MIGHT THEY RESPOND
TO THIS PRAYER?
WHAT WOULD THEY SHARE
TO SUPPORT YOUR
HEALING PROCESS?

LETTING GO
OF THE
HURT.

Holy Spirit,
you know before I ever ask
what assistance
is required.

I am acutely aware
of
pain,
sorrow,
regret,
second guessing,
denial,
aggravation and,
at times,
a desire for revenge.

These feelings need
to be
felt.

They are not better
than
contentment,
joy,
resiliency,
compassion,
integrity
or exhilaration.

They are just different aspects
of the
diverse spectrum
of
powerful emotions
human experience
encompasses.

HELP ME,
SPIRIT,
TO
HARMLESSLY PROCESS
AND RELEASE
THOSE FEELINGS

**THAT
DO NOT SERVE
MY PEACE.**

**GIVE ME THE
CLARITY TO WISH
PEACE
AND HEALING
TO THOSE WHO HAVE
INJURED ME
IN ANY WAY.**

I forgive and release
for my benefit,
my peace
and freedom,
as much,
or more
than
for theirs.

Toxicity of emotions,
be gone!

I AM CHOOSING
TO BE
PATIENT
AND
STEADFAST
IN
WITNESSING
MY
EVOLVING
CONSCIOUSNESS.

I AM SO RICHLY BLESSED.

Amen.

HOW DOES THIS PRAYER
APPLY TO YOUR LIFE
RIGHT NOW?

WHAT EMOTIONS
AND DREAMS DOES
THIS BRING UP FOR
YOU?

How Would You Modify This Prayer in Your Own Words?

USING THIS PRAYER, WHAT IS ONE STEP YOU CAN DO TO TRANSFORM THE ABUSE YOU'VE ENDURED?

WHO HAVE BEEN
YOUR MOST INSPIRING
TEACHERS IN THIS LIFETIME?
HOW MIGHT THEY RESPOND
TO THIS PRAYER?
WHAT WOULD THEY SHARE
TO SUPPORT YOUR
HEALING PROCESS?

No More Second Guessing the Pain of the Past.

RECONNECT ME TO MY CONFIDENCE, LORD.

I am committing my energies and focus,
here and now,
to no longer second guessing
the pain of the past.

Though recent experiences may have
rocked my sense of being in the present
and disturbed my peace,

**I AM CHOOSING TO MAKE A NEW CHOICE,
MOMENT TO MOMENT,
NOW.**

Analyzing and rehashing the often
mystifying behaviors of a former partner,
family member
or acquaintance
can weigh my joyful buoyancy down.

I am not willing to drown in
obsessive,
sorrowful
thinking.

I am stronger and brighter than this.

Help me,
Spirit

SHOW ME THE BETTER WAY,
THE HIGHER PATH TO FREEDOM
FROM EMOTIONAL CONUNDRUMS.

I am willing to change.

I AM WELCOMING REVITALIZING
THOUGHTS,
BEHAVIORS
AND ACTIONS.

I AM RELEASING WHAT
NO LONGER SERVES
TO CO-CREATE WITH YOU,
A LIFE MORE FULFILLING
THAN EVER BEFORE.

HOW DOES THIS PRAYER
APPLY TO YOUR LIFE
RIGHT NOW?

WHAT EMOTIONS
AND DREAMS DOES
THIS BRING UP FOR
YOU?

How Would You Modify This Prayer in Your Own Words?

USING THIS PRAYER,
WHAT IS ONE STEP
YOU CAN DO
TO
TRANSFORM THE ABUSE
YOU'VE ENDURED?

WHO HAVE BEEN
YOUR MOST INSPIRING
TEACHERS IN THIS LIFETIME?
HOW MIGHT THEY RESPOND
TO THIS PRAYER?
WHAT WOULD THEY SHARE
TO SUPPORT YOUR
HEALING PROCESS?

Primed and Ready.

I am primed and ready to release old
attitudes once again,
as many times as necessary,
which would curtail my progress in ceasing
to look outside of myself for
acceptance,
nurturing,
kindness
or other support.

**CODEPENDENCY IS FUELED MIGHTILY
BY A
SECRET BELIEF
THAT I MAY NOT
BE ENOUGH
TO DEAL WITH LIFE,
OR MAY NOT DESERVE
ALL THE RICHNESS
LIFE AFFORDS ME.**

I am primed and ready to stare down
the antiquated notion
that anyone else's evaluation
is more relevant to my life
than my own.

This new-found reliance
on the

Divine Guidance within me
is liberating any other programming
from this,
or
any other,
life time.

I AM FREE.

I AM INTERDEPENDENT WITH OTHERS.

LIFE IS GOOD AND PERPETUALLY MOVING
ME INTO DEEPER TRUST AND FAITH.

I AM WELL- PROVIDED FOR.

I AM LOVE.

I AM SAFE.

DIVINE ORDER ASSURES THE
POSITIVE OUTCOMES
I AM GIVING THANKS FOR
HERE AND NOW.

How Does This Prayer Apply to Your Life Right Now?

What Emotions and Dreams Does This Bring Up for You?

How Would You Modify This Prayer in Your Own Words?

USING THIS PRAYER, WHAT IS ONE STEP YOU CAN DO TO TRANSFORM THE ABUSE YOU'VE ENDURED?

WHO HAVE BEEN
YOUR MOST INSPIRING
TEACHERS IN THIS LIFETIME?
HOW MIGHT THEY RESPOND
TO THIS PRAYER?
WHAT WOULD THEY SHARE
TO SUPPORT YOUR
HEALING PROCESS?

BRAVERY.

Holy Spirit,
I no longer wish
to **NEED** to be
brave.

Create in me
the miracle of knowing
that courage doesn't have
to be in
effect 24 hours a day

**EASE ME ONTO A
GENTLER PATH
OF PEACE.**

**GIVE ME
THE INVALUABLE GIFT
OF REST.**

Remind me that
as I
meditate,
pray,
embrace the insights
and revelations
from regular time
in the
silence,
calmness,
and the
ability
to attract
tranquil situations
and people,
increase naturally.

It just does.

**I NO LONGER NEED
OR
WANT DRAMA.**

**PEACE AND JOY
CARRY THEIR OWN
BEAUTIFUL EXCITEMENT.**

Thank You,
God.

I AM HOME.

How Does This Prayer Apply to Your Life Right Now?

What Emotions and Dreams Does This Bring Up for You?

How Would You Modify This Prayer in Your Own Words?

USING THIS PRAYER, WHAT IS ONE STEP YOU CAN DO TO TRANSFORM THE ABUSE YOU'VE ENDURED?

WHO HAVE BEEN
YOUR MOST INSPIRING
TEACHERS IN THIS LIFETIME?
HOW MIGHT THEY RESPOND
TO THIS PRAYER?
WHAT WOULD THEY SHARE
TO SUPPORT YOUR
HEALING PROCESS?

Even Desperation
Can Be
A
Blessing
Now.

Desperation is a forceful emotion
which can hold one
in a terrible grip
of
sorrow,
loneliness,
alienation
and
discouragement.

It is an emotion
which can leave
as swiftly
as it arrived.

DESPERATION BE GONE!

Enough sorrow,
enough regret
and endless
over-analyzing.

OH,
PRECIOUS SPIRIT,
REMIND MY HEART
OF THE
BIGGER LIFE VISION,
THE EXPANDING
AWARENESS
THAT NO MATTER
WHAT HAS BEEN
TAKEN AWAY,
HEALTHY IMPULSES
REMAIN,
HAPPIER DREAMS
CAN BECOME
MY NEW REALITIES.

Show me what else,
what better plan awaits
for my future,
so I learn
that even desperation
can be
a blessing
now.

I arrived on this earth
with a natural,
open receptivity
to joy,
love,
discovery,
beauty
and spontaneity.

Surely all these qualities
remain within.

I am open
to their resurfacing
as soon as possible.

Divine Time,
Divine Order
through
Divine Love!

How Does This Prayer Apply to Your Life Right Now?

What Emotions and Dreams Does This Bring Up for You?

HOW WOULD YOU MODIFY THIS PRAYER IN YOUR OWN WORDS?

USING THIS PRAYER,
WHAT IS ONE STEP
YOU CAN DO
TO
TRANSFORM THE ABUSE
YOU'VE ENDURED?

WHO HAVE BEEN
YOUR MOST INSPIRING
TEACHERS IN THIS LIFETIME?
HOW MIGHT THEY RESPOND
TO THIS PRAYER?
WHAT WOULD THEY SHARE
TO SUPPORT YOUR
HEALING PROCESS?

Healing
the
Mockery
of
Love.

A narcissistic relationship can make a
mockery of all that feels
loving,
life enhancing
and joy reinforcing.

My trust has been shaken.

My worldview has been rearranged.

My confidence in my own ability to discern
a safe,
from unsafe,
person has been slain.

**SHOW ME THE WAY TOWARD THE LIGHT OF
EMPOWERED KNOWING OF MY WHOLENESS,
HOLY SPIRIT.**

I am Your Child.

**CRADLE ME
IN YOUR
EVERLASTING SWEETNESS,
ERASING MY
UNCERTAINTY.**

Shift my resistant struggling
willfulness to surrendered cooperation
in
reviving my knowing
of interconnectedness
with the
Divine
in
everyone and everything.

How Does This Prayer Apply to Your Life Right Now?

What Emotions and Dreams Does This Bring Up for You?

HOW WOULD YOU MODIFY THIS PRAYER IN YOUR OWN WORDS?

USING THIS PRAYER,
WHAT IS ONE STEP
YOU CAN DO
TO
TRANSFORM THE ABUSE
YOU'VE ENDURED?

WHO HAVE BEEN
YOUR MOST INSPIRING
TEACHERS IN THIS LIFETIME?
HOW MIGHT THEY RESPOND
TO THIS PRAYER?
WHAT WOULD THEY SHARE
TO SUPPORT YOUR
HEALING PROCESS?

I Have Gone
Too Far
to
Backslide Now.

I have decided that
I am committed to progress.

I am moving forward in the consciousness
expanding within my being.

I am stepping into my joy,
my relief,
my certainty of faith,
my confidence borne of the truth that I am
God's Treasured Child.

My joy is my own responsibility.

**HEAVEN TRULY IS AN INNER REFLECTION
OF FAITH RENEWING PERPETUALLY.**

Let my actions and responses
all reflect this inviolable Truth
from this moment on.

In deep gratitude.

HOW DOES THIS PRAYER APPLY TO YOUR LIFE RIGHT NOW?

WHAT EMOTIONS AND DREAMS DOES THIS BRING UP FOR YOU?

How Would You Modify This Prayer in Your Own Words?

Using This Prayer, What is One Step You Can Do to Transform the Abuse You've Endured?

WHO HAVE BEEN
YOUR MOST INSPIRING
TEACHERS IN THIS LIFETIME?
HOW MIGHT THEY RESPOND
TO THIS PRAYER?
WHAT WOULD THEY SHARE
TO SUPPORT YOUR
HEALING PROCESS?

Perceptiveness.

One of the greatest gifts of being perceptive
is the ability to learn from all
conditions and situations

AM I,
SWEET SPIRIT,
HOLDING ONTO OLD BAGGAGE
FROM
RELATIVES,
TEACHERS,
FRIENDS,
BUSINESS CONNECTIONS,
WHOSE OWN LIFE EXPERIENCES
HAVE BEEN
TAKEN ON
BY ME?

If so, dear God,
I am very eager to harmlessly release any
burden,
sense of frustration,
failure or regret,
guilt or shame,
which is not truly mine.

It is work enough to healthily perceive my
own life's areas which can be
clearer,

lighter,
better....

It **IS** my human part to have crystal
clarity concerning
what is,
and,
isn't mine
to do.

It is **NOT** my life's ambition to let the
lines blur between other people's
baggage,
expectations,
neediness,
and my own healthy responsibilities
and
desires.

Remind me
gently,
please,
to hold this realization in my awareness
at all times.

Thank You,
God.

Amen.

How Does This Prayer Apply to Your Life Right Now?

What Emotions and Dreams Does This Bring Up for You?

HOW WOULD YOU MODIFY
THIS PRAYER IN YOUR
OWN WORDS?

Using This Prayer, What is One Step You Can Do to Transform the Abuse You've Endured?

WHO HAVE BEEN
YOUR MOST INSPIRING
TEACHERS IN THIS LIFETIME?
HOW MIGHT THEY RESPOND
TO THIS PRAYER?
WHAT WOULD THEY SHARE
TO SUPPORT YOUR
HEALING PROCESS?

Making Different Choices Changes My Outcomes.

In silent moments of peaceful
contemplation, clarity arises
within
my heart and soul.

MOTIVATED BY LOVE FOR SPIRIT,
I AM MAKING
NEW,
DIFFERENT
CHOICES
THAT AFFIRM THE INHERENT BEAUTY
OF
EVERY PERSON
WHO COMES
INTO MY LIFE,
EVERY
ANIMAL,
EACH LEAF,
SHELL,
ROCK,
CLOUD,
BREEZE,
FLOWER.

Beauty adorns my world.

**MY PERSPECTIVE CONTINUALLY EVOLVES
INTO BROADER GRACE
AS MY LOVE
FOR THE
MIRACULOUS OPPORTUNITY
HAVING THIS
BODY TEMPLE
HOUSING MY SOUL
AFFORDS
DAILY.**

I am renewed by the
overflow,
abundance
and tender
mercies showing up
in my days.

As I receive these blessings,
I am better able
to be a force
for
ever- expanding good
in the world.

Thank You,
Thank You,
Thank You,
Gracious and Loving God.

How Does This Prayer Apply to Your Life Right Now?

What Emotions and Dreams Does This Bring Up for You?

HOW WOULD YOU MODIFY THIS PRAYER IN YOUR OWN WORDS?

USING THIS PRAYER, WHAT IS ONE STEP YOU CAN DO TO TRANSFORM THE ABUSE YOU'VE ENDURED?

WHO HAVE BEEN
YOUR MOST INSPIRING
TEACHERS IN THIS LIFETIME?
HOW MIGHT THEY RESPOND
TO THIS PRAYER?
WHAT WOULD THEY SHARE
TO SUPPORT YOUR
HEALING PROCESS?

Overcoming Discouragement.

Is there anyone among us
who has been immune
to
discouragement?

Does any person escape times of
doubt,
insecurity,
harsh emotional storms
which rage like hurricane velocity winds
blowing through our minds?

Is any one person so totally enlightened
that they are in total faith about
Higher Purposes,
Divine Appointments,
and losses
being inevitable steppingstones
to ever greater gains?

Lessons and blessings
do often hide

in seemingly horrible situations,
which means our aligning with faith,
would appear illogical,
wrenching
and infuriating,
yet aligning with faith restores
a sense of balance.

SHOW ME YOUR WAYS,
LORD,
THAT I MIGHT PUT THE PUZZLE PARTS
OF MY LIFE
TOGETHER
WITH EVER MORE
GRACE,
EASE
AND
JOY.

YOUR INFINITE LOVE
RESTORES MY PEACE,
WHEN I INVITE
AND ALLOW IT
TO DO SO.

I have decided to let resistance abate,

TO MOVE MORE IN TANDEM
WITH ETERNAL TRUTH

**AND SEE THE VISION
YOUR UNCONDITIONAL ACCEPTANCE
SHOWERS
ON MY LIFE.**

No forcing…
allowing!

No more fixing what never was broken…
joining with my
Mother/Father Spirit of Absolute Good
in flow with the energy of love I am.

With this renewing
attitude,
success,
fulfillment
and peace
are mine.

May it be Your will.

Amen and Thank You.

How Does This Prayer Apply to Your Life Right Now?

What Emotions and Dreams Does This Bring Up for You?

How Would You Modify This Prayer in Your Own Words?

USING THIS PRAYER,
WHAT IS ONE STEP
YOU CAN DO
TO
TRANSFORM THE ABUSE
YOU'VE ENDURED?

WHO HAVE BEEN
YOUR MOST INSPIRING
TEACHERS IN THIS LIFETIME?
HOW MIGHT THEY RESPOND
TO THIS PRAYER?
WHAT WOULD THEY SHARE
TO SUPPORT YOUR
HEALING PROCESS?

DOUBT.

All through life
there are new situations
which can stimulate
old insecurities
and doubts
about ourselves.

New
career,
moves,
losses of friends,
births,
deaths,
family,
relocating to a new house,
town or city...
health issues...
Meeting a new prospective mate,
changes in financial status,
etc.

Each marvelous new change
is a gift
which can challenge
our confidence
that we are
worthy,
capable,
and energetic
enough
to accomplish
what is expected.

Please,
and Thank You God,
for the ever present reassurance
that I am abundantly provided
with more than enough
insight,
vitality,
intellect,
Divine Ideas
and guidance

to achieve and fulfill,
all that is mine
to be,
do,
and have!

Doubt
can insidiously creep
in even at the most
joyful times.

I know now that by choosing
to remember all the
numerous occasions
when Divine Mercy
was showered wherever needed
in my life,
and those connected with me,
my confidence can erase
doubts
instantaneously.

**THERE IS NO PLACE
WHERE DIVINE LOVE
IS ABSENT,
THEREFORE I AM,
AND WE ARE,
SAFE
ALL THE TIME.**

This consciousness
restores and reinvigorates
my being.

I am so blessed.

Amen.

HOW DOES THIS PRAYER APPLY TO YOUR LIFE RIGHT NOW?

WHAT EMOTIONS AND DREAMS DOES THIS BRING UP FOR YOU?

How Would You Modify This Prayer in Your Own Words?

USING THIS PRAYER, WHAT IS ONE STEP YOU CAN DO TO TRANSFORM THE ABUSE YOU'VE ENDURED?

WHO HAVE BEEN YOUR MOST INSPIRING TEACHERS IN THIS LIFETIME? HOW MIGHT THEY RESPOND TO THIS PRAYER? WHAT WOULD THEY SHARE TO SUPPORT YOUR HEALING PROCESS?

I am Rising
from the
Ashes of Denial.

Total Denial evolves
into partial denial
which transforms into awareness
and
embracing
a Higher Truth.

**I AM RISING EVER UPWARD
FROM THE
BURNT ASHES OF DENIAL
INTO THE
REALM
OF
EXQUISITE EXHILARATION.**

No obstacle can overwhelm
the
clarity,
favor
and
goodness
God is.

I am,
therefore,
**REAFFIRMING FREQUENTLY
THE ALIGNMENT WITH DIVINE WILL.**

Where would you have me serve, Lord?

Who would you have my life touch
with Love today?

What is the next right thing I can do now
to make this earth a more humane place?

Tell me,
Lord,
so I can choose,
moment by cherished moment,
to live the Universal Law
that as I sow,
so shall I reap.

May my sowing seeds of caring
reap benefits for the Highest Good
of all involved.

Thy Will be Done.

Amen.

How Does This Prayer Apply to Your Life Right Now?

What Emotions and Dreams Does This Bring Up for You?

How Would You Modify This Prayer in Your Own Words?

Using This Prayer, What is One Step You Can Do to Transform the Abuse You've Endured?

WHO HAVE BEEN
YOUR MOST INSPIRING
TEACHERS IN THIS LIFETIME?
HOW MIGHT THEY RESPOND
TO THIS PRAYER?
WHAT WOULD THEY SHARE
TO SUPPORT YOUR
HEALING PROCESS?

YES, LORD, YES TO WHATEVER IS ASKED OF MY DAYS AND NIGHTS IN SERVICE TO YOU.

YES,
LORD,
YES TO WHAT IS ASKED
OF MY DAYS
AND
NIGHTS
IN SERVICE TO
YOU.

With a new level of faith
I am growing in my quiet conviction
that **I AM WHERE I AM SUPPOSED TO BE,
DOING WHAT IS MEANT FOR ME TO DO.**

You,
Lord,
have given me reprieve after reprieve,
no matter what the
circumstances,
forgiven my error actions
and disappointing behaviors.

It is your forgiveness of me
which fuels my resolve
to learn from my past choices
and move ahead.

**I AM ARMED
WITH
HARD-WON
LIFE EXPERIENCE.**

I am now choosing,
as never before,
to use that experience wisely
and well as **ALL I NEED TO BE
WILDLY SUCCESSFUL
AND EFFECTIVE
IS
WITHIN ME ALREADY.**

I am so happily blessed.

All is well with my soul today.

Thank You,
God.

Amen.

How Does This Prayer Apply to Your Life Right Now?

What Emotions and Dreams Does This Bring Up for You?

How Would You Modify This Prayer in Your Own Words?

Using This Prayer, What is One Step You Can Do to Transform the Abuse You've Endured?

WHO HAVE BEEN
YOUR MOST INSPIRING
TEACHERS IN THIS LIFETIME?
HOW MIGHT THEY RESPOND
TO THIS PRAYER?
WHAT WOULD THEY SHARE
TO SUPPORT YOUR
HEALING PROCESS?

ABUSE FALLOUT.

**THE ONLY PERSON
WHO IS CAPABLE
OF
HOLDING ME BACK
IS ME.**

Abuse fallout
can be so devastating
to my beliefs,
my self-assurance,
that I may temporarily
have played
into the
crazy notion
that I cannot
be,
do
and have
the love,
the career,

home,
friendships,
or,
family,
I desire.

**ABUSE FALLOUT
IS NOW BEING
REPLACED
BY THE
NATURAL FLOW
OF
DIVINE ORDER
IN MY
LIFE
AND AFFAIRS.**

Oh,
Lord,
Thank You
for
keeping me afloat
even when it felt
like
I was drowning.

Thank You for cleansing
my mind,
body
and spirit
of outmoded voices
damning my hopes,
denigrating my plans.

**AS YOUR BELOVED CHILD,
I AM INHERENTLY
DESERVING
OF A LOVE
WHICH
IS
HEALTHY,
MUTUALLY ATTRACTED,
ENCOURAGING,
UPLIFTING
AND
DEVOTED.**

In faith,
I replace abuse fallout
by rising
in the
Love of Spirit.

I am recognizing
how much I've learned from
the blessings
and gifts received
by knowing
that never again
will I settle
for anything less
than the treatment
all of us deserve.

I AM GRATEFUL AND WILLING
TO RELEASE THE
PAIN OF A PAST
I REPLACE
WITH
OPTIMISM,
RENEWAL
AND
REDIRECTED ENERGY
BORNE OF UNSHAKABLE
FAITH.

Thank You,
God.

Amen.

How Does This Prayer Apply to Your Life Right Now?

What Emotions and Dreams Does This Bring Up for You?

How Would You Modify This Prayer in Your Own Words?

USING THIS PRAYER, WHAT IS ONE STEP YOU CAN DO TO TRANSFORM THE ABUSE YOU'VE ENDURED?

WHO HAVE BEEN
YOUR MOST INSPIRING
TEACHERS IN THIS LIFETIME?
HOW MIGHT THEY RESPOND
TO THIS PRAYER?
WHAT WOULD THEY SHARE
TO SUPPORT YOUR
HEALING PROCESS?

CHAPTER 6

PEACE IS MINE.

PEACE
IS
MY
TRUE NATURE.

There is an endless wellspring of
benevolence flowing through my
life now.

This benevolence
is not based in material
acquisition or
ego-based score keeping.

This goodness is emblematic
of wishing more joyful loving,
more inner harmony
and comfort for all,
even those who have behaved in
erratic,
unpredictable,
unkind,
and dishonest ways.

I am,
in my Love of God,

becoming immune to the lower vibrations
of people who may not be ready to choose
a new path,
a more loving journey
through relationships.

What others do
no longer sets my ecstasy level,
no longer crushes my goals,
dreams
or ability
to simply **BE PEACE**.

**I AM PEACE
BECAUSE PEACE
IS MY TRUE NATURE.**

**I AM LOVE
BECAUSE LOVE
IS MY TRUE NATURE.**

I live this Truth
day to day.

In profound gratitude.

May the blessings be.

How Does This Prayer
Apply to Your Life
Right Now?

What Emotions
and Dreams Does
This Bring Up for
You?

How Would You Modify This Prayer in Your Own Words?

Using This Prayer, What is One Step You Can Do to Transform the Abuse You've Endured?

WHO HAVE BEEN
YOUR MOST INSPIRING
TEACHERS IN THIS LIFETIME?
HOW MIGHT THEY RESPOND
TO THIS PRAYER?
WHAT WOULD THEY SHARE
TO SUPPORT YOUR
HEALING PROCESS?

I Am Retrieving
My Inner
Container
of
Joy
for
My Peace
and
Healing.

May I be a far better container
for the
harmony and peace
I've missed so much.

Impermanence dictates
the perpetual changes
from one moment,
one season,
and one decade
to another.

It is all perfectly
in
Divine Order.

It is all
a splendid manifestation
of the
Universal Mind.

I am an integral part
of the whole.

Though I've forgotten this
in the heat of
dysfunctional events,
places,
people,
pressures,
I now choose to remember
the
Higher Truth
of
who I am.

I came here
to be
peace,
joy,
kindness,
and love
in action and at rest.

**I AM NO LONGER
WILLING
TO ALLOW ANYONE'S
BEHAVIOR,
ATTITUDES
OR
VALUES
TO
DISTRACT ME
FROM
MY PEACE.**

Peace is mine.

Joy is mine.

Discernment is mine.

Lasting relief
from suffering
is mine.

Thank You,
Spirit.

How Does This Prayer Apply to Your Life Right Now?

What Emotions and Dreams Does This Bring Up for You?

How Would You Modify This Prayer in Your Own Words?

Using This Prayer, What is One Step You Can Do to Transform the Abuse You've Endured?

WHO HAVE BEEN
YOUR MOST INSPIRING
TEACHERS IN THIS LIFETIME?
HOW MIGHT THEY RESPOND
TO THIS PRAYER?
WHAT WOULD THEY SHARE
TO SUPPORT YOUR
HEALING PROCESS?

MY PEACE COMES, LIKE EVERY OTHER BLESSING, FROM THE GOD WHO IS MORE THAN ENOUGH.

THERE IS A SECRET LANGUAGE
DIVINE LOVE
SPEAKS
WHICH IS UNIQUELY PREPARED
FOR EACH
LISTENER.

I REALIZE,
LORD,
IT IS MY HUMAN PART
TO RECOGNIZE THAT MESSAGE
AS
HEAVEN-SENT.

YOU ARE EVER WITH ME.

WE ARE UNITED.

This awareness,
understanding
and Truth
ARE the inviolable pact
You have made
as
my,
our,
Mother/Father Spirit.

My peace,
then,
doesn't depend on outer manifestations
of other people's
attention,
approval,
affection
or companionship.

**MY PEACE IS NOT
DEPENDENT
ON OUTER
HONORS,
TROPHIES,
GIFTS,
TITLES,
WEATHER,**

**FINANCIAL WEALTH,
AREA I LIVE IN,
CAR I DRIVE,
CLOTHING I WEAR...**

My peace comes,
like every other blessing,
from the
**GOD WHO
IS MORE
THAN
ENOUGH.**

God,
Thank You
for being
my unending Source
of everything
beautiful,
real,
loving
and true.

I AM CALMNESS.

I AM HARMONY.

I AM STEADINESS.

I AM DEVOTION.

I AM EQUANIMITY.

I AM BALANCE.

I AM RADIANT LOVE IN

ACTION. I AM <u>THAT</u>, I AM.

I AM TRULY <u>THAT</u>, I AM.

How Does This Prayer Apply to Your Life Right Now?

What Emotions and Dreams Does This Bring Up for You?

HOW WOULD YOU MODIFY THIS PRAYER IN YOUR OWN WORDS?

Using This Prayer, What is One Step You Can Do to Transform the Abuse You've Endured?

WHO HAVE BEEN
YOUR MOST INSPIRING
TEACHERS IN THIS LIFETIME?
HOW MIGHT THEY RESPOND
TO THIS PRAYER?
WHAT WOULD THEY SHARE
TO SUPPORT YOUR
HEALING PROCESS?

CHAPTER 7

PASSION
AND
ENTHUSIASM.

ENERGY,
ONCE SQUANDERED
ON
APPREHENSIVENESS,
NOW IS DEVOTED
TO
RECEIVING
WONDERFUL NEW
WAYS TO THRIVE,
SHARE
AND CO~CREATE
WILD,
OFTEN, INNOVATIVE
IDEAS.

I am standing on
sacred ground
wherever I go.

**THE PRESENCE
OF THE
DIVINE
IS EVERYWHERE.**

**THE HEALING BALM
OF
CONSCIOUSLY TRUSTING
LIFE'S UNFOLDING EVENTS
FREES
MY MIND.**

Energy,
once squandered
on
apprehensiveness,
now is devoted
to
receiving
wonderful new ways
to thrive,
share
and co-create
wild,
often, innovative
ideas.

Where there may have seemed
only blocked doors,

**NOW THE DOORS SWING OPEN WIDE
FOR ME.**

I am ready
to cherish
the sacred ground
everywhere apparent.

I am consciously
looking to find people
behaving compassionately.

I am embracing their inherent holiness
as well as
my own.

Sitting in the silence
assists my ability
to hear inner direction
being revealed,
old insecurities
being organically healed.

**EMPOWERED BY DIVINE LOVE,
I AM ALIGNED
WITH THE**

**LIFE FORCE,
AND AM PART
OF THE
UNENDING CHAIN
OF
BLESSING.**

All is well.

Amen.

How Does This Prayer Apply to Your Life Right Now?

What Emotions and Dreams Does This Bring Up for You?

How Would You Modify This Prayer in Your Own Words?

Using This Prayer, What is One Step You Can Do to Transform the Abuse You've Endured?

WHO HAVE BEEN
YOUR MOST INSPIRING
TEACHERS IN THIS LIFETIME?
HOW MIGHT THEY RESPOND
TO THIS PRAYER?
WHAT WOULD THEY SHARE
TO SUPPORT YOUR
HEALING PROCESS?

Prayer
for
Revitalizing
Passion.

You always know my wishes,
Spirit,
before I speak or write,
before I think or sing,
dance,
stretch
into new arenas
of hope.

Life's demands can exhaust
my enthusiasm
and
sap my energy.

Remind me,
Lord,
of the bigger vision,
the inevitability
of a
Higher Truth

always working toward the direction
of
evolution
and growth.

There is revitalizing passion
for
living with
peace,
integrity,
love,
patience,
compassion,
faith
and zeal
when I choose to remember
all of this.

**KEEP RECONNECTING ME
TO MY ZEAL.**

Thank you for reminding me
again and again
of the
identity I own
beyond

my given name,
fingerprints,
street address,
etc.

Because I am
Your Beloved Child,
I am heir
to the energy
you fire.

How Does This Prayer Apply to Your Life Right Now?

What Emotions and Dreams Does This Bring Up for You?

How Would You Modify This Prayer in Your Own Words?

Using This Prayer, What is One Step You Can Do to Transform the Abuse You've Endured?

WHO HAVE BEEN
YOUR MOST INSPIRING
TEACHERS IN THIS LIFETIME?
HOW MIGHT THEY RESPOND
TO THIS PRAYER?
WHAT WOULD THEY SHARE
TO SUPPORT YOUR
HEALING PROCESS?

Inherent
Value.

My inherent worth
cannot be devalued
by anyone.

It is a Divine Gift
given as birthright.

**I WILL NO LONGER DIGNIFY
THE
ERRONEOUS THOUGHTS,
OR
BEHAVIORS,
OF
ANOTHER PERSON.**

There is no validity,
and I will not be reduced
based on
"less than values and opinions".

I am Your Beloved Child.

This inviolable Truth frees me
from all small mindedness,
petty accusations,
and differences

445

in cultural,
societal,
or,
personal
judgments.

I am answering to a Higher Truth,
an ever expanding consciousness
of Love,
benevolent intention,
clarity of purpose,
and acceptance
of the
rich gifts
already appropriated
for me
in this lifetime.

**AS MY OWN CONSCIOUSNESS EXPANDS,
I AM RECEIVING EVER HAPPIER
RELATIONSHIPS,
EVEN GREATER
PEACE,
HARMONY,
GUIDANCE,
AND SIMPLICITY.**

All is well.

I give grateful honor
to the
Divine Presence
within and all around me.

How Does This Prayer Apply to Your Life Right Now?

What Emotions and Dreams Does This Bring Up for You?

How Would You Modify This Prayer in Your Own Words?

Using This Prayer, What is One Step You Can Do to Transform the Abuse You've Endured?

WHO HAVE BEEN
YOUR MOST INSPIRING
TEACHERS IN THIS LIFETIME?
HOW MIGHT THEY RESPOND
TO THIS PRAYER?
WHAT WOULD THEY SHARE
TO SUPPORT YOUR
HEALING PROCESS?

Restore My Zeal, Please, Holy Spirit.

There is no spot
devoid of the Divine,
no matter what
the physical scene may be.

Have I become so discouraged,
so exhausted by abuse,
that I have lost my zeal for living?

Help me move forward,
Lord,
beyond the self-limiting confines
of a
broken dream,
a defeatist attitude.

You made me for better than this.

**YOU CREATED ME
TO BE
A UNIQUE REFLECTION
OF
YOUR PERFECTION.**

My enthusiasm can return,
zeal for the adventure of what is new,
what is next
can take center stage.

I am ready and receptive
to my good.

Thank You,
Lord.

How Does This Prayer Apply to Your Life Right Now?

What Emotions and Dreams Does This Bring Up for You?

How Would You Modify This Prayer in Your Own Words?

USING THIS PRAYER,
WHAT IS ONE STEP
YOU CAN DO
TO
TRANSFORM THE ABUSE
YOU'VE ENDURED?

WHO HAVE BEEN
YOUR MOST INSPIRING
TEACHERS IN THIS LIFETIME?
HOW MIGHT THEY RESPOND
TO THIS PRAYER?
WHAT WOULD THEY SHARE
TO SUPPORT YOUR
HEALING PROCESS?

Let There Be Light.

Wherever people are feeling lost,
may their purpose and direction
be revealed
to them.

May they pause long enough
to ask for guidance,
and know clearly
how to proceed.

Let there **be** Light,
and there **was** Light.

Wherever
hunger,
pollution,
famine,
war,
disease,

and unrest
dominate the landscape,
may the peace
of
Divine Love
intervene.

May gratitude
and harmony
be reestablished
in each
mind,
heart,
body,
and soul.

Let there BE Light,
and
there WAS Light.

May each moment
of our lives
be lived as choice
to see
the
Divine Light

and Abundance
in everyone and everything.

**MAY PEACE BE REALIZED
ON EVERY LEVEL...**

Let there **BE** Light,
and
there **IS** Light.

Amen
and
Thank You,
Lord.

HOW DOES THIS PRAYER APPLY TO YOUR LIFE RIGHT NOW?

WHAT EMOTIONS AND DREAMS DOES THIS BRING UP FOR YOU?

How Would You Modify This Prayer in Your Own Words?

Using This Prayer, What is One Step You Can Do to Transform the Abuse You've Endured?

WHO HAVE BEEN
YOUR MOST INSPIRING
TEACHERS IN THIS LIFETIME?
HOW MIGHT THEY RESPOND
TO THIS PRAYER?
WHAT WOULD THEY SHARE
TO SUPPORT YOUR
HEALING PROCESS?

Enthusiasm.

**TO BE ENTHUSED
MEANS "ENTHEOS",
TO BE INFUSED
WITH THE
DIVINE.**

I am,
you are,
we are,
infused with enthusiasm
for the
life
we are privileged to live,
the
people,
animals,
and
opportunities
which abound.

BLESSINGS ARE EVERYWHERE.

**IT'S MY RESPONSIBILITY
TO NOTICE THEM.**

I am an enthusiastic participant
in sharing my own goodness
with everyone
I encounter.

No meeting is by accident.

**EVERYONE
IS
MY TEACHER
AS I AM
A WILLING TEACHER
FOR THEM.**

May it be Your Will,
Infinite Creator,
that I remember
the truth
of this reality
in every interaction
today,
and
always.

Thy Will be Done.

How Does This Prayer Apply to Your Life Right Now?

What Emotions and Dreams Does This Bring Up for You?

How Would You Modify This Prayer in Your Own Words?

USING THIS PRAYER, WHAT IS ONE STEP YOU CAN DO TO TRANSFORM THE ABUSE YOU'VE ENDURED?

WHO HAVE BEEN
YOUR MOST INSPIRING
TEACHERS IN THIS LIFETIME?
HOW MIGHT THEY RESPOND
TO THIS PRAYER?
WHAT WOULD THEY SHARE
TO SUPPORT YOUR
HEALING PROCESS?

I Am Intending to Do Soul~Enriching Activities Daily for My Transformed Life.

Knowing the choice is mine
where I choose
to direct my attention,
I am intending
to do
soul enriching activities.

These activities become the
foundation for my
spiritual practices.

My life is transformed,
moment
by
sacred moment,

as I take my power,
based on gratitude
for the
universe
of infinite blessings
in my life
and affairs, back.

**I AM NO LONGER POSTPONING
MY JOY,
PEACE,
CENTEREDNESS.**

**FULFILLMENT IS ALREADY
MINE.**

Gratitude
creates profound peace
through
my love for the God
who is more
than
enough.

All is abundantly
overflowing with
tender mercies.

With full awareness
of these
unlimited blessings,
I am maintaining
a state of grace
in
each breath inhaled,
each encounter with nature's majesty,
every person I interact with.

**THANK YOU,
LORD
FOR THE
HOLY EXPERIENCE
MY DAILY LIFE
IS.**

Amen.

How Does This Prayer Apply to Your Life Right Now?

What Emotions and Dreams Does This Bring Up for You?

How Would You Modify This Prayer in Your Own Words?

Using This Prayer, What is One Step You Can Do to Transform the Abuse You've Endured?

WHO HAVE BEEN
YOUR MOST INSPIRING
TEACHERS IN THIS LIFETIME?
HOW MIGHT THEY RESPOND
TO THIS PRAYER?
WHAT WOULD THEY SHARE
TO SUPPORT YOUR
HEALING PROCESS?

GENEROSITY
OF
SPIRIT.

Because life
is an
ever-renewing journey
of
twists and turns,
detours and quests,
we sometimes
may have found ourselves
on pot-holed roads,
or
veered off the highway into
a muddy creek.

**IN THOSE DEEP VALLEY
TIMES
IT IS OUR CHANCE
TO DEMONSTRATE
GENEROSITY OF SPIRIT
TO OURSELVES –**
scarred,
tossed,

lost,
and unsure
as we may be,
we are still perfect
in our imperfection.

Are we ever the only ones
who experience
sorrow,
alienation,
uncertainty,
rejection,
misery
of inner resistance
to necessary changes?

Haven't we observed
others' triumphs
back into the irresistible
Light of faith,
devotion,
reinvigoration,
and transmutation of regret
into positive resolve?

Show me the way,
the smoother path,

so my energy may be freer,
my heart lighter,
and my creativity expanded.

**MAY GENEROSITY OF SPIRIT
BE MY
INNER GIFT
TO
MYSELF FIRST,
THEN SHARED WITH
EVERY SOUL
I KNOW IN SERVICE
TO THE
ONE POWER AND PRESENCE,
MY ROCK AND REDEEMER.**

Amen.

How Does This Prayer Apply to Your Life Right Now?

What Emotions and Dreams Does This Bring Up for You?

How Would You Modify This Prayer in Your Own Words?

Using This Prayer, What is One Step You Can Do to Transform the Abuse You've Endured?

WHO HAVE BEEN
YOUR MOST INSPIRING
TEACHERS IN THIS LIFETIME?
HOW MIGHT THEY RESPOND
TO THIS PRAYER?
WHAT WOULD THEY SHARE
TO SUPPORT YOUR
HEALING PROCESS?

My Identity
Is Now Rooted
in an
Unerring Alignment
with
God's Love.

Unerring alignment
with God's Love
fuels my passion
for
life and living.

My identity as soul
is now rooted
in that understanding.

If that knowing is challenged
by another's
confusion,
anger,
hurt,
fear,
accusation,
or complaint,
I go within.

I do a reality check,
a consciously chosen process
of conferring
with the
Indwelling Presence
to enlighten me
about both
the
others' perceptions
and my own.

It isn't a question ultimately
of who is right
and who is wrong.

The question is always: what is
**THE MOST LOVING AND COMPASSIONATE
APPROACH
TO ASSUMING EACH ENCOUNTER
IS AN HONORING
OF THE
DIVINE LIGHT
WITHIN EACH
OF US?**

How can we each feel cherished?

How can we clear fear away,
to reveal the core love
which wishes
to be
in the forefront!

With this approach,
we stay on an aligned path
of gentle,
and steadfast
sacredness.

We are strong.

BUOYED UP BY CORE VALUES
WHICH CELEBRATE MY
CAPACITY
FOR
RESILIENCY,
I AM ENTHUSED ABOUT
THE CONSTRUCTIVE
SHIFTS,
RELEASES
AND
PASSION
FOR LIFE
RETURNING TO ME
NOW.

All blessings arise
from the tender mercies
of
my
Source.

How generous,
compassionate
and cherishing
is my Gracious
and Loving God.

How Does This Prayer Apply to Your Life Right Now?

What Emotions and Dreams Does This Bring Up for You?

How Would You Modify This Prayer in Your Own Words?

Using This Prayer, What is One Step You Can Do to Transform the Abuse You've Endured?

WHO HAVE BEEN
YOUR MOST INSPIRING
TEACHERS IN THIS LIFETIME?
HOW MIGHT THEY RESPOND
TO THIS PRAYER?
WHAT WOULD THEY SHARE
TO SUPPORT YOUR
HEALING PROCESS?

LET ME CHOOSE
A NEW APPROACH,
LORD.
I AM
TREMENDOUSLY
WILLING
TO
MOVE FORWARD
GRACEFULLY
NOW.

Let my life become realized anew
as a meditation in motion,
a moving prayer
of
compassionate intention.

I am living in service
to the
One Presence and Power
so generous,
so attuned

to my constructive wants
and desires,
that no blight on my past,
no failed project or relationship
can shatter my optimism.

This is my new approach.

There is only room here
for blessing,
for revelation of greatness,
awareness of loving kindness
given and received.

I asked to choose a new path.

I AM
TREMENDOUSLY WILLING
TO KEEP MOVING FORWARD
GRACEFULLY.

NO LOSS OR SACRIFICE
OF THE PAST
CAN BIND ME
ANYMORE.

May it be Your Will.

Thank You,
God.

Amen.

.

How Does This Prayer Apply to Your Life Right Now?

What Emotions and Dreams Does This Bring Up for You?

HOW WOULD YOU MODIFY THIS PRAYER IN YOUR OWN WORDS?

Using This Prayer, What is One Step You Can Do to Transform the Abuse You've Endured?

WHO HAVE BEEN
YOUR MOST INSPIRING
TEACHERS IN THIS LIFETIME?
HOW MIGHT THEY RESPOND
TO THIS PRAYER?
WHAT WOULD THEY SHARE
TO SUPPORT YOUR
HEALING PROCESS?

CHAPTER 8
BLESSINGS ABOUND, SHIFTS ARE HAPPENING NOW.

ABUNDANT
FINANCIAL PROSPERITY
IS
MINE.

**YES,
TO MY RENEWED,
EXPANDED FINANCIAL WELL-BEING
NOW!**

Yes,
to trusting Divine Inspiration
infuses me
with clear knowing
about who to connect with,
how to function effectively,
where to go,
what specific direction
will
advance my vision.

I am engaged
in bringing heaven down
to earth
by knowing,
and,
acknowledging
the
Divine Order
everywhere present.

ALL IS WELL WITH MY SOUL.

My marching orders arise
from the
unshakable conviction
that God
is my
personal,
professional
orchestrator.

**AS GOD'S BELOVED CHILD,
I AM TRULY HEIR
TO THE
KINGDOM OF INFINITE
INTELLIGENCE
SHOWING UP
GRACEFULLY.**

I am inviting
the wisdom,
judgment,
patience,
integrity,
imagination
and stamina
to flow through
and around,
me and everyone
I connect with.

Used to blessing myself
and others
in caring,
joyful ways,
I am delighted to experience
abundant fulfillment
financially,
and in all ways.

May it be Your Will,
Lord.

Thank You,
Thank You,
Thank You.

Amen.

HOW DOES THIS PRAYER APPLY TO YOUR LIFE RIGHT NOW?

WHAT EMOTIONS AND DREAMS DOES THIS BRING UP FOR YOU?

How Would You Modify This Prayer in Your Own Words?

Using This Prayer, What is One Step You Can Do to Transform the Abuse You've Endured?

WHO HAVE BEEN
YOUR MOST INSPIRING
TEACHERS IN THIS LIFETIME?
HOW MIGHT THEY RESPOND
TO THIS PRAYER?
WHAT WOULD THEY SHARE
TO SUPPORT YOUR
HEALING PROCESS?

Standing
in a
Higher Principle
Now.

Remembering the salvation
of
Divine Compensation,
my consciousness rises
like a phoenix
from the ashes
of
sadness,
loss,
anger,
blame,
rejection
and
confusion.

I am victorious
over self-defeating decisions
and yearnings.

I am leaping forward
in the
vindication of success

I am a Beloved Child
of Truth.

All is in
Divine Right Order,
now,
always was,
always will be.

I cannot be moved
from this
consciousness of wellness,
emboldened
by an
energy of silent trust
that my life is guided Divinely
all the while.

Thank You,
Goddess,
Thank You.

How Does This Prayer Apply to Your Life Right Now?

What Emotions and Dreams Does This Bring Up for You?

How Would You Modify This Prayer in Your Own Words?

USING THIS PRAYER, WHAT IS ONE STEP YOU CAN DO TO TRANSFORM THE ABUSE YOU'VE ENDURED?

WHO HAVE BEEN
YOUR MOST INSPIRING
TEACHERS IN THIS LIFETIME?
HOW MIGHT THEY RESPOND
TO THIS PRAYER?
WHAT WOULD THEY SHARE
TO SUPPORT YOUR
HEALING PROCESS?

PRAYER
FOR
INTEGRITY.

Keeping my word,
whether anyone else does,
or,
not,
is not always an easy task.

Like an angered child,
I feel sometimes that if those around me
don't follow through,
why should I?

Why can't I just operate at their level?

Why must I go out of my way
to be my best,
live in integrity?

Help me,
Lord,
to realign
with your will
of taking the High Road regardless of
what other paths
a partner,
a family member,
a child,
a friend,
or co-worker
may choose.

I KNOW WE ALL WALK
ON OUR OWN
SOUL'S PATH.

I AM ANSWERING
TO THE
DIVINE SOURCE
WITHIN
ME.

I HAVE DECIDED
THAT LIVING
AT THE
HIGHEST STANDARD
IN
WORD,
THOUGHT
AND
DEED
IS A PRIVILEGE.

Taking the High Road
feels good,
not in a sanctimonious way.

It feels good to live a clean day
untarnished by
deceit,
dishonesty
and sneakiness
or thievery.

MY CONSCIENCE IS MY
RENEWED GUIDE;
THAT STILL,
SMALL VOICE
WITHIN WHICH
FORMS A
BLESSED MORAL COMPASS
I CAN COUNT ON
ALWAYS.

How Does This Prayer Apply to Your Life Right Now?

What Emotions and Dreams Does This Bring Up for You?

How Would You Modify This Prayer in Your Own Words?

Using This Prayer, What is One Step You Can Do to Transform the Abuse You've Endured?

WHO HAVE BEEN YOUR MOST INSPIRING TEACHERS IN THIS LIFETIME? HOW MIGHT THEY RESPOND TO THIS PRAYER? WHAT WOULD THEY SHARE TO SUPPORT YOUR HEALING PROCESS?

A LIFE LIVED
DRAMA
AND
CLUTTER~FREE.

What if every day
of the rest of my life
can be
easy,
simple,
loving,
joyful?

What a concept.

What an intention.

I am running with this intentional way
to approach
every moment
with
renewed ease.

**I AM CHOOSING TO KEEP EVERY MOTION,
EACH SHARED PARTICIPATION
AS SIMPLE AS POSSIBLE,
DRAMA AND CLUTTER-
FREE.**

I have decided
to be loving to God,
to myself
and
everyone I encounter.

I AM A FUNDAMENTALLY JOYFUL ENTITY
EXPERIENCING
THE
PRIVILEGE
OF
LIVING LIFE.

JOY IS INHERENT
IN MY
NATURE.

My happiness is a natural result
of
noticing what is
gentle,
kind,
colorful,
graceful,
merciful
and authentic in
nature,
other people
and animals,
and in my own character.

THANK YOU,
SPIRIT,
FOR MAKING A WORLD
OF
INFINITELY IMAGINATIVE
FORM.

Amen.

.

How Does This Prayer Apply to Your Life Right Now?

What Emotions and Dreams Does This Bring Up for You?

How Would You Modify This Prayer in Your Own Words?

USING THIS PRAYER, WHAT IS ONE STEP YOU CAN DO TO TRANSFORM THE ABUSE YOU'VE ENDURED?

WHO HAVE BEEN
YOUR MOST INSPIRING
TEACHERS IN THIS LIFETIME?
HOW MIGHT THEY RESPOND
TO THIS PRAYER?
WHAT WOULD THEY SHARE
TO SUPPORT YOUR
HEALING PROCESS?

THE POWER
OF
DECISION.

Decisions need to be made,
Lord.

Isn't it high time
for a
new road?

Hasn't the pile-up
of
pain,
the abuse,
disappointment,
and the confusion
of feeling lost burdened my life
long enough?

There is power
in being still
and recognizing

this critically relevant fact
which motivates me
to take a time apart
from the rush and pull
of daily life.

**I AM LISTENING
TO THE
STILL,
SMALL
VOICE
WITHIN
WHOSE MESSAGES ARE INHERENTLY
REASSURING,
COMPASSIONATE
AND
ENCOURAGING.**

I am choosing
a new,
improved way
to be,
aware that the word disappointment
means not a divine,
or,
fitting appointment
anymore.

I have decided to
feel the regrets,
process the emotions,
harmlessly release the hurts,
and regain my joyful nature
now.

No more harm
is allowed.

**I WAS NEVER PUT
ON THIS EARTH
TO SUFFER.**

Surely,
it is a perversion
of love
if someone maltreats another.

**I HAVE DECIDED TO ALIGN
MY WILL
WITH THE
DIVINE WILL.**

**DECISION MAKING
IS
EMPOWERING
AND
LIBERATING.**

I am offering so much gratitude
for guidance
which infuses my life with
new,
healthier,
light-hearted
beliefs.

**I AM MADE
IN THE
BENEFICENT ILLUMINATION
OF MY
GRACIOUS
AND
COMPASSIONATE GOD'S
INFINITELY
PATIENT,
COMFORTING
ENFOLDMENT.**

**TENDER MERCIES
AND
DIVINE GRACE
ARE MINE.**

May I share them well.

Amen.

How Does This Prayer Apply to Your Life Right Now?

What Emotions and Dreams Does This Bring Up for You?

HOW WOULD YOU MODIFY THIS PRAYER IN YOUR OWN WORDS?

USING THIS PRAYER,
WHAT IS ONE STEP
YOU CAN DO
TO
TRANSFORM THE ABUSE
YOU'VE ENDURED?

WHO HAVE BEEN
YOUR MOST INSPIRING
TEACHERS IN THIS LIFETIME?
HOW MIGHT THEY RESPOND
TO THIS PRAYER?
WHAT WOULD THEY SHARE
TO SUPPORT YOUR
HEALING PROCESS?

I Am
Choosing
to
Look Within
for
Renewal
and
Guidance.

If the outer world
of
daily responsibilities and obligations,
relationships and work life
feels somewhat overwhelming,
I am learning to become
still.

I AM CHOOSING TO GO WITHIN,
GIVING GREAT GRATITUDE
FOR THE GUIDANCE
WHICH HEALS,
THE NEW DIRECTIONS
WHICH RENEW MY SENSE
OF PURPOSE
AND PASSION

**FOR
LIVING.**

I am never at a loss
for what to be,
do
and have
when my focus remains
on the
Divine Order
of
God's love
everywhere available
all the time.

I now remember
that this
Eternal Truth
refutes dark thoughts,
and helps ancient destructive patterns
to leave now.

Thank You,
God,
for
renewal and guidance.

Amen.

How Does This Prayer Apply to Your Life Right Now?

What Emotions and Dreams Does This Bring Up for You?

How Would You Modify This Prayer in Your Own Words?

Using This Prayer,
What is One Step
You Can Do
to
Transform the Abuse
You've Endured?

WHO HAVE BEEN
YOUR MOST INSPIRING
TEACHERS IN THIS LIFETIME?
HOW MIGHT THEY RESPOND
TO THIS PRAYER?
WHAT WOULD THEY SHARE
TO SUPPORT YOUR
HEALING PROCESS?

HEALTHY
DETACHMENT
LEADS
TO
HEALTHY LOVING.

**I AM LEARNING,
BELOVED SPIRIT,
THAT DETACHING HEALTHILY
FROM
A TOXIC SITUATION
DOES NOT RENDER ME
UNCARING
OR
ALOOF.**

It leads me back to
my priorities being lived
from
**A CONSCIOUSNESS
OF CHOICE.**

It frees my heart
to focus
on the
Source of All,
the God

544

who is more
than
enough.

It invites me
to pay close attention
to my relationship
with my own cherished
Body Temple,
mind
and Eternal Soul.

It renews and revitalizes
my once dim awareness
that I am inherently
strong,
vital
and invaluable
because I am
God's Beloved Child,
heir to all that's good.

THANK YOU,
SPIRIT,
FOR HEALTHY DETACHMENT:
THE GIFT OF HONORING
MY BIRTHRIGHT
TO
PEACE,
FREEDOM,
COMPASSION,
EMPATHY
AND
CONNECTION.

Amen.

.

How Does This Prayer Apply to Your Life Right Now?

What Emotions and Dreams Does This Bring Up for You?

How Would You Modify This Prayer in Your Own Words?

USING THIS PRAYER, WHAT IS ONE STEP YOU CAN DO TO TRANSFORM THE ABUSE YOU'VE ENDURED?

WHO HAVE BEEN
YOUR MOST INSPIRING
TEACHERS IN THIS LIFETIME?
HOW MIGHT THEY RESPOND
TO THIS PRAYER?
WHAT WOULD THEY SHARE
TO SUPPORT YOUR
HEALING PROCESS?

AWARENESS
IS THE
GREATEST FRIEND
OF
POSITIVE CHANGE.

Reconnect me
to my clear vision
of myself
as a
full,
vibrantly alive
human,
Lord.

Drained by
repeating patterns
of
pain,
lost dreams,
shattered ideas
of what relationships can be,

I no longer wish
to flounder aimlessly.

DON'T LET ME BE ADRIFT ANYMORE.

**BE MY HARBOR,
HEAVENLY MOTHER/FATHER.**

**HELP ME ACCEPT
WHAT CANNOT BE CHANGED**
in someone else,
as my own life force energy
redirects
towards You,
towards me.

This has been a long time in the making.

May the insights,
Lessons
and blessings
come to me soon
and lastingly.

I feel your Everlasting Embrace
as the ship of my existence
moves further along
on a windswept ocean,
soothed by the balm
of
resurrected calmness.

How Does This Prayer Apply to Your Life Right Now?

What Emotions and Dreams Does This Bring Up for You?

How Would You Modify This Prayer in Your Own Words?

USING THIS PRAYER,
WHAT IS ONE STEP
YOU CAN DO
TO
TRANSFORM THE ABUSE
YOU'VE ENDURED?

WHO HAVE BEEN
YOUR MOST INSPIRING
TEACHERS IN THIS LIFETIME?
HOW MIGHT THEY RESPOND
TO THIS PRAYER?
WHAT WOULD THEY SHARE
TO SUPPORT YOUR
HEALING PROCESS?

EQUANIMITY: NATURE TEACHES US TO ENDURE STORMS AS WELL AS FLOURISH IN CALM WATERS.

Nature is life itself.
It is not bad or good.
It just **is**.

I am so aware,
moment to moment,
of the gift
nature constantly bestows
by
demonstrating the diversity
of living.

I am open
and receptive
not only to the blessing
of a peaceful sunrise.

I am open
to the
pounding surf's uneven waves,
the turmoil embodied in
blizzards,
tornados,
etc...

Like the energy moving
through
my emotional body,
change is continual.

**I AM EMBRACING
THE ELEGANCE
OF
CHANGE.**

**I AM EMBODYING THE
RENEWAL
OF POSSIBILITY,
NO LONGER SHROUDED
BY RESTRICTIVE IDEAS
WHICH CAN
SHATTER DREAMS.**

**I AM EXPANSIVELY ALIVE
IN AN
EVER-EVOLVING
CONSCIOUSNESS.**

Change is my friend
as the wind blows seeds
to grow
new trees,
flowers,
shrubs.

Thank You,
Spirit,
for sharing your infinite creations
in wondrous forms
and magnificent ways.

AWE TOUCHES MY HEART DAILY!

Amen.

How Does This Prayer Apply to Your Life Right Now?

What Emotions and Dreams Does This Bring Up for You?

How Would You Modify This Prayer in Your Own Words?

USING THIS PRAYER, WHAT IS ONE STEP YOU CAN DO TO TRANSFORM THE ABUSE YOU'VE ENDURED?

WHO HAVE BEEN
YOUR MOST INSPIRING
TEACHERS IN THIS LIFETIME?
HOW MIGHT THEY RESPOND
TO THIS PRAYER?
WHAT WOULD THEY SHARE
TO SUPPORT YOUR
HEALING PROCESS?

ONLY LOVE
SPOKEN HERE.

God,
I desire to live
where
only love is spoken,
only compassion
is welcomed
to the
dinner table,
only mutual joy
and committed passion
occurs in the bedroom.

God,
instruct me how to live
in such a way,
live at such a standard
of pure intention
that no one will darken my door
who isn't able
to meet me fully.

I am ready to be shown
my human part.

I am willing to coexist
with any dark shadows
of my past,
or present,
to co- create with You,
the perfect setting
for
miraculous shifts.

Thank You,
God,
for being
the
Reassurer,
my
Rock and Redeemer.

**IN YOUR LOVE
THE GROUND IS LAID
FOR ALL
THE OTHER LOVES
OF MY LIFE.**

Amen.

.

How Does This Prayer Apply to Your Life Right Now?

What Emotions and Dreams Does This Bring Up for You?

HOW WOULD YOU MODIFY
THIS PRAYER IN YOUR
OWN WORDS?

Using This Prayer, What is One Step You Can Do to Transform the Abuse You've Endured?

WHO HAVE BEEN
YOUR MOST INSPIRING
TEACHERS IN THIS LIFETIME?
HOW MIGHT THEY RESPOND
TO THIS PRAYER?
WHAT WOULD THEY SHARE
TO SUPPORT YOUR
HEALING PROCESS?

CHAPTER 9

FAITH
IS
ITS OWN REWARD.

Reaching Out
to Others
for
Help.

I have felt
reluctance
and
resistance
to
requesting help:
Emotionally
Physically
Financially
Professionally.

There has been a fear
of
appearing
needy,
seeming weak,
losing another's respect.

Whatever fears echo
in my consciousness
from
societal pressures,

parent's messages,
condemning voices,
I say a resounding "yes"
to the
Divine Presence
showing me a new way
to be.

A better time is a hand
where fine help
is asked for,
or,
offered,
and received gracefully
by me.

People who help me
are given the privilege
of being of service,
of using their aptitudes
and skills
in constructive ways.

This is a joyful opportunity
for us both.

AS I REVITALIZE
AND STRENGTHEN,
I,
TOO,
DELIGHT IN GIVING.

GIVING IS RECEIVING.

RECEIVING IS GIVING.

Both are in Divine Flow,
and I am gratefully
evolving.

Thanks be
to the
One Love.

How Does This Prayer Apply to Your Life Right Now?

What Emotions and Dreams Does This Bring Up for You?

How Would You Modify This Prayer in Your Own Words?

USING THIS PRAYER, WHAT IS ONE STEP YOU CAN DO TO TRANSFORM THE ABUSE YOU'VE ENDURED?

WHO HAVE BEEN
YOUR MOST INSPIRING
TEACHERS IN THIS LIFETIME?
HOW MIGHT THEY RESPOND
TO THIS PRAYER?
WHAT WOULD THEY SHARE
TO SUPPORT YOUR
HEALING PROCESS?

THE
DIVINE PLAN
LIBERATES
MY LIFE.

**IF ONE PERSON
REJECTS,
DISCARDS,
DEMEANS,
LIES TO,
STEALS FROM
OR CHEATS
ON ME,
IT IS A REFLECTION
OF THAT INDIVIDUAL'S
CHARACTER ONLY.**

NOT MINE!

I am reaffirming
that there are
lessons,
blessings
and huge gifts
possible from all of this.

**I AM NO LONGER WILLING
TO BE MALTREATED
BY ANYONE
FOR ANY REASON...
ESPECIALLY NOT
IN THE NAME
OF LOVE.**

I am God's Beloved Child
with **ABSOLUTELY NOTHING TO PROVE**,
and am becoming free
of my list
of
regrets and shame.

It is a new day
dawning for my life.

**THE DIVINE PLAN
IS REVEALING ITSELF
TO ME
AND I FOLLOW THIS LEAD
TO THE
GARDEN OF EDEN
WHICH AWAITS.**

Some days
my heart has felt
like a desert,
parched and hopelessly
bereft of fruit and flowers.

Now I trust
the oasis
is at hand.

The steps I take,
the inner reflection,
the refocusing of energy
and devotion
to
Divine Order
is occurring.

This all strengthens
my resolve
to remain undefeatable.

The Lord is on my side.

**I AM FREE
IN MY
ETERNAL SOUL.**

All is well,
now and always.

How Does This Prayer Apply to Your Life Right Now?

What Emotions and Dreams Does This Bring Up for You?

How Would You Modify This Prayer in Your Own Words?

USING THIS PRAYER, WHAT IS ONE STEP YOU CAN DO TO TRANSFORM THE ABUSE YOU'VE ENDURED?

WHO HAVE BEEN
YOUR MOST INSPIRING
TEACHERS IN THIS LIFETIME?
HOW MIGHT THEY RESPOND
TO THIS PRAYER?
WHAT WOULD THEY SHARE
TO SUPPORT YOUR
HEALING PROCESS?

Discouragement
Leaves!

Discouragement leaves
as I affirm my knowing
that all good,
every blessing,
comes from
the One Presence
and Power.

God's love
revives my hope
through my ever-deepening
faith.

No room is left
for
depression,
self-rejection,
blame,

shame
or grievances
when I acknowledge
the
overflow,
abundance
and more than enough
reasons to rejoice
daily.

HERE,
NOW,
PERPETUALLY,
I AM CONSCIOUS
OF UNLIMITED TIDES
OF GIFTS
FLOWING
INTO MY LIFE
EASILY
AND IN
MERCIFUL WAYS.

Thy will be done.

Thanks be
to the
Divine Love
that
God is.

Amen.

How Does This Prayer
Apply to Your Life
Right Now?

What Emotions
and Dreams Does
This Bring Up for
You?

How Would You Modify This Prayer in Your Own Words?

USING THIS PRAYER, WHAT IS ONE STEP YOU CAN DO TO TRANSFORM THE ABUSE YOU'VE ENDURED?

WHO HAVE BEEN
YOUR MOST INSPIRING
TEACHERS IN THIS LIFETIME?
HOW MIGHT THEY RESPOND
TO THIS PRAYER?
WHAT WOULD THEY SHARE
TO SUPPORT YOUR
HEALING PROCESS?

FORGETTING
THE
DIVINE TRUTH
NO MORE!

Even though there is always
a part of my heart
so attuned
to the Truth
that You,
God,
are the only game in town,
the One Presence and Power
evenly available
to
everyone,
everywhere,
no exceptions....
I sometimes forget...

I have fallen prey,
in my past,

to people's misguided concepts
and been swayed
from my full faith.

This has led
to pain,
to a vision of lack
and separation.

Reconnect me
to the
Divine Truth,
the unerring Link
which is
my Inner Compass,
my True North.

What knowing
could assure
more peace,
freedom
and healthy relationships?

**I AM READY,
WILLING AND EAGER
TO REPLACE
OLD LIES
WITH
ETERNAL TRUTHS.**

I am **THAT**, I am.

I truly am
embracing **THAT**,
I am.

Thanks be to God.

Amen.

.

How Does This Prayer Apply to Your Life Right Now?

What Emotions and Dreams Does This Bring Up for You?

HOW WOULD YOU MODIFY THIS PRAYER IN YOUR OWN WORDS?

USING THIS PRAYER, WHAT IS ONE STEP YOU CAN DO TO TRANSFORM THE ABUSE YOU'VE ENDURED?

WHO HAVE BEEN
YOUR MOST INSPIRING
TEACHERS IN THIS LIFETIME?
HOW MIGHT THEY RESPOND
TO THIS PRAYER?
WHAT WOULD THEY SHARE
TO SUPPORT YOUR
HEALING PROCESS?

I Am Embracing Miraculous Shifts Now!

There were times I came
to believe my ideas,
needs,
preferences
were irrelevant.

I **BELIEVED** that I did not count.

I was
a
mere pinpoint
on the tapestry
of life.

My choices and ability
to attract
healthily suffered.

I believed a lie of insignificance,
"not enoughness"
of
love,

compassion,
kindness,
attention,
nourishment,
emotional sustenance,
etc...

How do I discard and dismantle
these antiquated core issues
which led to
believing in
abandonment,
betrayal,
and rejection?

I am preparing
for a new reality
to embrace
the loving kindness,
the tender Benevolence
God is.

**NOW IS THE BLESSED MOMENT
OF
MIRACULOUS SHIFTS.**

I am ready.

I HAVE DECIDED
THE OLD
MUST BE LET GO
IN FAVOR OF RENEWAL,
RECLAIMING MY TRUE
DIVINE NATURE
IN PARTNERSHIP
WITH ALL
THAT IS TRUE,
ALL THAT IS LOVING,
AND ALL
THAT IS
LIFE-AFFIRMING.

Thank you,
Energy of Life,
for this
extraordinary awareness
of
expanding
consciousness
of
Your Presence.

I am returning
to the
loving being
you created me
to be,
moment to moment,
breath by precious breath.

I give thanks,
and move on
in
peace and faith.

Amen.

How Does This Prayer Apply to Your Life Right Now?

What Emotions and Dreams Does This Bring Up for You?

How Would You Modify
This Prayer in Your
Own Words?

.

USING THIS PRAYER,
WHAT IS ONE STEP
YOU CAN DO
TO
TRANSFORM THE ABUSE
YOU'VE ENDURED?

WHO HAVE BEEN
YOUR MOST INSPIRING
TEACHERS IN THIS LIFETIME?
HOW MIGHT THEY RESPOND
TO THIS PRAYER?
WHAT WOULD THEY SHARE
TO SUPPORT YOUR
HEALING PROCESS?

HELP ME LIVE
IN THE
NOW,
GODDESS,
PLEASE.

Tightness is borne
of pain
around
past
or future.

Apprehension causes anxiety.

I no longer am available
for sorrow,
worry,
and suffering.

I am now giving deep thanks
for relief and release
of,

what once appeared intractable,
from
inner negativities.

I intend to bless
and help myself
and everyone
around me.

The old has passed by.

**THE FUTURE HOLDS
ALL THE PROMISE
I AM OPEN TO.**

One can never measure
the power of intention
to spread understanding
in
one's own heart,
and share with others.

**MY PRESENT MOMENT
IS A
GEM OF ACCEPTANCE.**

I am very awakened
to the
Light
living
within me,
within all,
here,
now
eternally.

I am
THAT,
I am.

I am
THAT,
I am.

I truly am
THAT,
I am.

Amen.

How Does This Prayer Apply to Your Life Right Now?

What Emotions and Dreams Does This Bring Up for You?

How Would You Modify This Prayer in Your Own Words?

Using This Prayer, What is One Step You Can Do to Transform the Abuse You've Endured?

WHO HAVE BEEN
YOUR MOST INSPIRING
TEACHERS IN THIS LIFETIME?
HOW MIGHT THEY RESPOND
TO THIS PRAYER?
WHAT WOULD THEY SHARE
TO SUPPORT YOUR
HEALING PROCESS?

Leap of Faith.

Days sometimes arrive
in my
reclaiming process,
where I feel
lost,
rudderless
and
exhausted.

On those days,
it may feel hard
to nurture the child
who
breathes within.

Heal me at depth,
Holy Spirit,
and remind those parts
which feel bereft,
feel like love
has bypassed my heart...

**BEFORE I CALL,
YOUR PRESENCE
WARMS,**

SURROUNDS
AND
ENFOLDS
ME.

Doubts recede,
no matter how strong
my resistance rises like firecrackers
on the 4th of July.

They burn out
because your Illuminating Love
is balm
to my soul.

There is only
Love.

How Does This Prayer
Apply to Your Life
Right Now?

What Emotions
and Dreams Does
This Bring Up for
You?

How Would You Modify This Prayer in Your Own Words?

USING THIS PRAYER,
WHAT IS ONE STEP
YOU CAN DO
TO
TRANSFORM THE ABUSE
YOU'VE ENDURED?

WHO HAVE BEEN
YOUR MOST INSPIRING
TEACHERS IN THIS LIFETIME?
HOW MIGHT THEY RESPOND
TO THIS PRAYER?
WHAT WOULD THEY SHARE
TO SUPPORT YOUR
HEALING PROCESS?

FAITH
IS AN
ANCHOR
IN
EVEN THE
MOST TURBULENT
SEAS.

**FULL ACCEPTANCE IN THE HEART = FAITH.
FAITH IS MY ANCHOR
IN EVEN THE MOST SEEMINGLY TURBULENT
SEAS WHEN THE BOAT OF MY LIFE
APPEARS TO BE
ADRIFT.**

Floating along without direction,
on chaotic currents and changing tides
could terrify me
if I allowed it
to make me anxious.

My faith that there is
Divine Direction
active in every situation

allows my thoughts
to be
resourceful,
calm,
creatively,
and vitally
alive
with potential.

**I AM GUIDED
HOW TO HELP CLEAR AWAY
ALL OBSTACLES
TO MY GOOD.**

Tides and destructive winds
cease to push the boat of my life
as I listen to the reassurance
of Spirit
within whispering Guidance.

A CALM SEA FLOATS INSIDE MY HEART.

**PEACE,
SOLACE,
AND CONTENTMENT
LIVE,**

**BREATHE,
AND SUSTAIN
MY JOY MORE
EACH HOUR.**

Thanks be
to the
One Presence
and
Power.

Amen.

How Does This Prayer Apply to Your Life Right Now?

What Emotions and Dreams Does This Bring Up for You?

HOW WOULD YOU MODIFY THIS PRAYER IN YOUR OWN WORDS?

Using This Prayer, What is One Step You Can Do to Transform the Abuse You've Endured?

WHO HAVE BEEN
YOUR MOST INSPIRING
TEACHERS IN THIS LIFETIME?
HOW MIGHT THEY RESPOND
TO THIS PRAYER?
WHAT WOULD THEY SHARE
TO SUPPORT YOUR
HEALING PROCESS?

HOLY SPIRIT, OVERRIDE MY DOUBT WITH HOPE.

The God
who is
more than
enough
enables me to
transcend,
transmute
and transform
no matter how disconnected,
how deep the chasm
between
what is wished for
and what appears to have
manifested.

There is no adversary powerful enough
to oppose

the
Infinite Brilliance
and
Absolute Purity
of
God.

**THE
ONE PRESENCE
AND
POWER
OVERWHELMS ALL DOUBTS,
ERADICATES ALL
RESENTMENTS AND FEARS
BECAUSE I HAVE ASKED
FOR THIS
PROFOUND HEALING
TO OCCUR.**

Nothing I've invited
is impossible.

No one is broken.

**HOPE AND UPLIFTMENT
SUPERSEDES
EVEN THE REMOTEST
POTENTIAL
FOR
FAILURE.**

Divine Order assures
I am,
we all are,
where we need to be,
right here
and
now.

Thy Will be done.

Amen.

How Does This Prayer
Apply to Your Life
Right Now?

What Emotions
and Dreams Does
This Bring Up for
You?

HOW WOULD YOU MODIFY THIS PRAYER IN YOUR OWN WORDS?

Using This Prayer, What is One Step You Can Do to Transform the Abuse You've Endured?

WHO HAVE BEEN
YOUR MOST INSPIRING
TEACHERS IN THIS LIFETIME?
HOW MIGHT THEY RESPOND
TO THIS PRAYER?
WHAT WOULD THEY SHARE
TO SUPPORT YOUR
HEALING PROCESS?

I Am Ready
to
Have My Faith
Renewed.

Faith shattered leads
to hopelessness
and feelings of
loneliness,
emptiness
and often, excessive neediness.

Faith renewed
and restored
leads to a quiet knowing
that all is happening
precisely as it needs to
for lessons and blessings
to be appreciated
and applied.

Having experienced the
pain,
sorrow,

grief
of faith
interrupted by cynicism,
resentment and/or temporary depression,
I HAVE DECIDED TO MAKE A NEW CHOICE.

Like a flower
pushing towards the sun's
healing,
nourishing
light,
despite several
seemingly unfavorable
conditions of
wind,
water,
or soil,
I AM NOW READY TO RENEW MY FAITH.

Faith restored lays the foundation
for
inner calm,
for the fertile soil
of
loving kindness,

a sense of my interconnectedness
with
all of life.

FAITH IS A CHOICE,
JUST AS HAPPINESS IS BORNE
OF A WILLINGNESS
TO RETURN
TO THE
ABILITY
TO GO WITHIN,
BE STILL ENOUGH,
LONG ENOUGH,
TO HEAR INFINITE BLESSING,
ULTIMATE WISDOM
AND BE SHOWN
A NEW WAY
OF
INNER PEACE
NOW.

REMIND ME TO KEEP MY
RESOLVE
STRONG,
HOLY SPIRIT.

I am ready to explore
peace,
faith
and
serenity

one moment at a time.

Thy Will be done.

How Does This Prayer
Apply to Your Life
Right Now?

What Emotions
and Dreams Does
This Bring Up for
You?

How Would You Modify This Prayer in Your Own Words?

Using This Prayer, What is One Step You Can Do to Transform the Abuse You've Endured?

WHO HAVE BEEN
YOUR MOST INSPIRING
TEACHERS IN THIS LIFETIME?
HOW MIGHT THEY RESPOND
TO THIS PRAYER?
WHAT WOULD THEY SHARE
TO SUPPORT YOUR
HEALING PROCESS?

MY ANCHOR
IN
EVERY WEATHER.

Tossed adrift
by life's inequities,
I sometimes may feel
like a floundering boat
adrift,
rudderless.

You be my anchor,
Lord,
when instability
seems to obscure
my sense
of
Your Presence.

Send Angels and Ascended Masters
to my side.

Comfort comes
from the sweet benevolence
You are.

Though thoughts
of lack and resistance
come unbidden,
I know they are of the ego
gripping my heart.

The ego fights
my expanding conscious awareness
in my
Divine Nature
to thwart me
from attempting too much
that is unknown,
thus far.

The ego seeks to keep me alive
and safe
from harm,
yet it cannot be allowed
to kill my dreams
and wondrous progress
toward renewal

of knowing
peace is mine,
and
grace is given
freely.

JUBILANCE IN ALL AREAS
OF MY LIFE
IS LIKELY
AS I TURN ALL OUTCOMES
OVER TO GOD'S CARE
AND KEEPING.

I rest in the knowledge
of this safe harbor.

ALL IS IN DIVINE FLOW.

THE BLESSINGS ARE MIRACULOUS.

No enemy can overcome
the
One Presence
and
Power
equally available to me,
to all,
all the time.

HOW DOES THIS PRAYER
APPLY TO YOUR LIFE
RIGHT NOW?

WHAT EMOTIONS
AND DREAMS DOES
THIS BRING UP FOR
YOU?

HOW WOULD YOU MODIFY
THIS PRAYER IN YOUR
OWN WORDS?

USING THIS PRAYER, WHAT IS ONE STEP YOU CAN DO TO TRANSFORM THE ABUSE YOU'VE ENDURED?

WHO HAVE BEEN
YOUR MOST INSPIRING
TEACHERS IN THIS LIFETIME?
HOW MIGHT THEY RESPOND
TO THIS PRAYER?
WHAT WOULD THEY SHARE
TO SUPPORT YOUR
HEALING PROCESS?

ANGELS MUST BE ASKED
ASKED
BECAUSE
I HAVE FREE WILL.

Reconnect me
to my Guardian Angels,
Holy Spirit.

**I AM ASKING
BECAUSE I KNOW ANGELS
WILL NEVER IMPOSE
THEIR ASSISTANCE
ON HUMANS.**

Show me,
please,
these inspired connections
abounding
with
Divine Ideas,
healing concepts,
powerful synchronicities.

I am asking because
to try to do things
from just
my "human will"
has caused
suffering and sorrow.

I am available
for
Angelic Healing
which
guides,
directs
and renews
my sense
of
innocence and wonder.

Thank You,
Holy Spirit,
for the
wellspring
of
Infinite Love
that I perceive
now.

How Does This Prayer
Apply to Your Life
Right Now?

What Emotions
and Dreams Does
This Bring Up for
You?

How Would You Modify This Prayer in Your Own Words?

USING THIS PRAYER,
WHAT IS ONE STEP
YOU CAN DO
TO
TRANSFORM THE ABUSE
YOU'VE ENDURED?

WHO HAVE BEEN
YOUR MOST INSPIRING
TEACHERS IN THIS LIFETIME?
HOW MIGHT THEY RESPOND
TO THIS PRAYER?
WHAT WOULD THEY SHARE
TO SUPPORT YOUR
HEALING PROCESS?

STAND WITH ME, HOLY SPIRIT.

Holy Spirit,
Divine Supporter and Restorer
of
inner peace and comfort,
stand with me
today.

Arch Angels,
Angels,
Ascended Masters
and Ancestors,
be mighty
in the midst
of my
reclaiming process
now.

Areas
of
unclarity and sadness,
confusion and self-rejecting concepts...

BE GONE FROM MY CONSCIOUS
AND
SUB-CONSCIOUS.

Help me remember
that the
Infinite Intelligence
that God is
has need of my determination
to live my best life,
share the Light of Divine Love
with everyone I meet,
reach beyond shyness,
fear of being judged inadequate,
to my truly empowered reality
as a
treasured child
of the
Divine.

This is my Truth.

No other Truth can contradict
my wholeness,
wellness
or
inherent dignity.

Exaggerations and lies
foisted on me
about
life being anguish producing,
or
love being hurtful,
or
suffering being the main feeling
in
relationships too exhausting to endure,
BE GONE!

In their
place,
comfort,

acceptance,
ease,
grace,
laughter,
creativity,
bliss,
purposeful guidance
easily heard,
integrity and compassionate loving...
REIGN SUPREME!

Amen.

How Does This Prayer Apply to Your Life Right Now?

What Emotions and Dreams Does This Bring Up for You?

How Would You Modify This Prayer in Your Own Words?

Using This Prayer, What is One Step You Can Do to Transform the Abuse You've Endured?

WHO HAVE BEEN
YOUR MOST INSPIRING
TEACHERS IN THIS LIFETIME?
HOW MIGHT THEY RESPOND
TO THIS PRAYER?
WHAT WOULD THEY SHARE
TO SUPPORT YOUR
HEALING PROCESS?

Turning It All Over to Spirit.

Remind me,
Holy Spirit,
to release the insistence
on everything
being the way
I want it to be
right away.

Impatience is borne
of a fearfulness
that I'll run out of
energy,
resolve,
time,
"stick-to-it-ness",
etc...

Let my impetus
come from love,
and remember that patience
with the process
of
evolving into a new view
is worthy of whatever
it takes.

I AM NOT RUNNING A RACE.

I AM CO-CREATING
WITH YOUR INFINITE LOVE
GUIDING EVERY STEP,
A NEW,
FINER CONSCIOUSNESS.

I am becoming clearer
as a channel
for giving and receiving
love at an
elevated level.

I am becoming new
through being renewed
by Spirit.

**I AM EXACTLY ON TIME
BECAUSE MY LIFE
AND AFFAIRS ARE,
BY CHOICE,
RUNNING
ON
DIVINE TIME.**

Remind me,
Lord,
if my old thoughts
tug occasionally away
from the
High Road,
and try to waylay
my determination.

With your
Unwavering Guidance,
I am safe.

Thank You,
God.

Amen.

How Does This Prayer Apply to Your Life Right Now?

What Emotions and Dreams Does This Bring Up for You?

How Would You Modify This Prayer in Your Own Words?

USING THIS PRAYER, WHAT IS ONE STEP YOU CAN DO TO TRANSFORM THE ABUSE YOU'VE ENDURED?

WHO HAVE BEEN
YOUR MOST INSPIRING
TEACHERS IN THIS LIFETIME?
HOW MIGHT THEY RESPOND
TO THIS PRAYER?
WHAT WOULD THEY SHARE
TO SUPPORT YOUR
HEALING PROCESS?

WITH FAITH, ALL SHIFTS IN BELIEF CAN OCCUR.

Depression has been defined
as
anger turned inward.

Anger is the result
of
fearful feelings and doubts
about how to get one's needs met.

**WITH FAITH,
ALL MIRACULOUS SHIFTS
IN
BELIEF
CAN OCCUR.**

**I AM DESIRING
MIRACULOUS SHIFTS
RIGHT NOW,
RIGHT HERE.**

674

**SHIFTS TOWARD SELF-REGARD,
PUTTING MY RELATIONSHIP
WITH THE
DIVINE SOURCE
AHEAD OF
ANY HUMAN RELATIONSHIP...**

When this is established firmly,
I focus on my own relationship
with myself.

Have I managed
to be truly
loving,
caring,
nurturing
and protective
of my
Inner Child's needs?

**AM I PROTECTIVE,
COMPASSIONATE
AND DEVOTED**

TO MY
INNER CHILD
CURRENTLY?

What can I resolve to do
to be fully committed
to reparenting
my earlier ages
in
compassionate,
caring ways?

I am committed
to providing myself
organic food,
clean water,
clothes,
safe and comfortable housing,
excellent bedding,
healthy recreation,
livelihood
with
loyal,
functional

true friends,
family,
love,
creative expression,
meditation,
prayer time,
gratefulness
and faith.

What are the best activities
for
nurturing myself
on this
blessed day?

Am I deeply breathing in
the Light and Love of God,
or am I inhaling
shallowly,
unconsciously blocking
the
Life Force Energy

as I take in
the energy of air?

Am I fully exhaling,
intending to let go harmlessly
of whatever no longer serves
my life's joy and purposes?

Remind me gently,
Beloved Spirit,
of these basic truths
so I may serve myself
and
Your other
cherished daughters
and sons,
in service
to
You.

The blessings endure.

**MY PEACE IS ARRIVING
IN
INCREDIBLY WONDROUS
WAYS.**

I AM READY.

Thank You,
Beloved Spirit
of
Life.

Amen.

How Does This Prayer Apply to Your Life Right Now?

What Emotions and Dreams Does This Bring Up for You?

How Would You Modify This Prayer in Your Own Words?

USING THIS PRAYER,
WHAT IS ONE STEP
YOU CAN DO
TO
TRANSFORM THE ABUSE
YOU'VE ENDURED?

WHO HAVE BEEN
YOUR MOST INSPIRING
TEACHERS IN THIS LIFETIME?
HOW MIGHT THEY RESPOND
TO THIS PRAYER?
WHAT WOULD THEY SHARE
TO SUPPORT YOUR
HEALING PROCESS?

CHAPTER 10
THE LIGHT LEADS THE WAY.

WHAT WE DEFINE, WE TEND TO LIMIT.

Do we ever really allow ourselves
permission
to fully know
another?

Are we often so reluctant
to risk reaching out
to another
that we define people
by
job,
race,
gender,
religion,
socio-economics,
and
geography?

WHAT WE DEFINE,
WE TEND
TO LIMIT
IN OUR
PERCEPTION.

THE DIVINE
PRESENCE
VIEWS ALL
AS
THE LOVE
THEY ARE,
THE
PERSONIFICATION
OF
GRACE.

Why would I,
as a
Beloved Child
of the
Great Spirit,
do less?

Affirmative Prayer:

I AM WILLING AND
EAGER
TO VIEW EVERYONE,
INCLUDING MYSELF,
AS SOUL,
AS THE
MANIFESTATION
OF THE

DIVINE
IN
BODILY FORM.
I AM NOW WILLING
TO LET GO
OF
PAST OUTER
JUDGMENTS
AND SEE
THE
DIVINE LIGHT
IN EACH PERSON.

In this endeavor
I give thanks
for the
privilege
of
practicing
the
Presence,
moment to moment.

Thank You,
God.

How Does This Prayer Apply to Your Life Right Now?

What Emotions and Dreams Does This Bring Up for You?

How Would You Modify This Prayer in Your Own Words?

USING THIS PRAYER,
WHAT IS ONE STEP
YOU CAN DO
TO
TRANSFORM THE ABUSE
YOU'VE ENDURED?

WHO HAVE BEEN
YOUR MOST INSPIRING
TEACHERS IN THIS LIFETIME?
HOW MIGHT THEY RESPOND
TO THIS PRAYER?
WHAT WOULD THEY SHARE
TO SUPPORT YOUR
HEALING PROCESS?

LET THERE BE LIGHT.

Wherever people
are feeling lost,
may their purpose
and direction
be revealed to them.

May they pause long enough
to ask for guidance,
and know clearly
how to proceed.

Let there **BE** Light,
and there **WAS** Light.

Wherever
hunger,
pollution,
famine,
war,
disease,
and unrest
dominate the landscape,

may the peace
of
Divine Love
intervene.

May gratitude
and harmony
be reestablished in each
mind,
heart,
body,
and soul.

Let there **BE** Light,
and there **WAS** Light.

May each moment
of our lives
be lived as choice
to see
the Divine Light
and Abundance
in everyone
and everything.

MAY PEACE BE REALIZED
ON EVERY LEVEL.

Let there BE Light,
and there IS Light.

Amen
and
Thank You,
Lord.

Affirmative Prayer:
WHEREVER THE ILLUSION
OF
DARKNESS
SEEMS TO DOMINATE,
I AM CHOOSING TO REMEMBER
THAT EVEN IN THAT MOMENT,
GOD IS WITH ALL,
AND ALL IS WELL,
NOW
AND
ALWAYS.

**I AM SAFE,
ENFOLDED
IN THE
LOVING AND PROTECTIVE
ARMS
OF
DIVINE GRACE.**

Peace is my birthright.
I claim it
now.

Amen.

How Does This Prayer Apply to Your Life Right Now?

What Emotions and Dreams Does This Bring Up for You?

How Would You Modify This Prayer in Your Own Words?

Using This Prayer, What is One Step You Can Do to Transform the Abuse You've Endured?

WHO HAVE BEEN
YOUR MOST INSPIRING
TEACHERS IN THIS LIFETIME?
HOW MIGHT THEY RESPOND
TO THIS PRAYER?
WHAT WOULD THEY SHARE
TO SUPPORT YOUR
HEALING PROCESS?

DAILY QUIET REFLECTION.

In the push and strain
so many do engage in daily,
Lord,
remind me gently,
please,
to take a time of quiet reflection,
every single day.

Whether it's done on a beach,
in a park,
a home sanctuary space for prayer
and meditation,
a museum,
school
or,
house of worship,
I know
Your Divine Presence
pervades everything
and everyone.

That includes me
and everybody
else.

NO EXCEPTIONS.

Therefore,
I am relearning the significance
of daily reflection
on the
unlimited blessings
that fill
my life,
and the lives of others
all the time.

This time
of
quiet contemplation
reinforces my faith
and stimulates my
determination

to harmlessly release
negative ideas
and messages
from childhood.

Whether I was bullied
by
family members,
teachers
or clergy,
a bully in the cafeteria,
or abused sexually,
verbally,
physically,
or psychologically,
I am facing
the
Higher Truth
of
being redeemed
by
Divine Love
here and now.

I am **THAT**,
I am!

Amen.

How Does This Prayer Apply to Your Life Right Now?

What Emotions and Dreams Does This Bring Up for You?

HOW WOULD YOU MODIFY THIS PRAYER IN YOUR OWN WORDS?

Using This Prayer, What is One Step You Can Do to Transform the Abuse You've Endured?

WHO HAVE BEEN
YOUR MOST INSPIRING
TEACHERS IN THIS LIFETIME?
HOW MIGHT THEY RESPOND
TO THIS PRAYER?
WHAT WOULD THEY SHARE
TO SUPPORT YOUR
HEALING PROCESS?

THE IRRESISTIBLE POWER OF LIGHT.

Light shines
because its nature
is to shine.

I AM OF THE LIGHT,
THEREFORE
I WILL NO LONGER
ALLOW ANYONE,
OR,
ANY SITUATION,
TO DIMINISH
THE
LIGHT
I NATURALLY AM.

Reconnect me
to this
invincible
knowing,
Lord.

Remind me
that darkness goes back
to the nothingness
from whence it came
once
Light replaces it.

**I AM YOUR CHILD,
HEIR TO THE LIGHT
YOU ARE.**

The irresistible power
of
Divine Light
is
healing,
strengthening
and comforting
me
now.

Thank You,
Thank You,
Thank You,
  Lord.

  Amen.

How Does This Prayer Apply to Your Life Right Now?

What Emotions and Dreams Does This Bring Up for You?

How Would You Modify This Prayer in Your Own Words?

Using This Prayer, What is One Step You Can Do to Transform the Abuse You've Endured?

WHO HAVE BEEN
YOUR MOST INSPIRING
TEACHERS IN THIS LIFETIME?
HOW MIGHT THEY RESPOND
TO THIS PRAYER?
WHAT WOULD THEY SHARE
TO SUPPORT YOUR
HEALING PROCESS?

How Do We Discern Which Guidance Is Truly of the Light vs When It's Our Ego's Fearful Voice?

My narcissistic abuser
may have tried
to convince me
that I'd never have better
so I might as well settle
for crumbs.

Abusers do that
so to break down self-esteem
that there seems to be
no hope of another
lick at life.

They endeavor to wall one off
from
opportunity,
close optimism off
by
choking hope
into
submission.

**HELP ME,
GOD,
TO DISCERN BETTER,
EACH HOUR,
WHAT IS
OF
YOUR WISDOM
AND WHAT IS
THE EGO'S FEARFUL VOICE SAYING,
"SO FAR AND NO FURTHER."**

I AM SO READY TO IMPROVE,
so determined
not to wander
like a lost sheep.

I am living
in the fold
of
Divine Love
and am reinforcing
this
Truth,
moment to moment.

Amen.

How Does This Prayer Apply to Your Life Right Now?

What Emotions and Dreams Does This Bring Up for You?

How Would You Modify This Prayer in Your Own Words?

USING THIS PRAYER, WHAT IS ONE STEP YOU CAN DO TO TRANSFORM THE ABUSE YOU'VE ENDURED?

WHO HAVE BEEN
YOUR MOST INSPIRING
TEACHERS IN THIS LIFETIME?
HOW MIGHT THEY RESPOND
TO THIS PRAYER?
WHAT WOULD THEY SHARE
TO SUPPORT YOUR
HEALING PROCESS?

Evening Prayer To Honor the Day Now Past, and Prepare for an Outstanding Rest Overnight, and Blessed Day Tomorrow.

Beloved Spirit,
I am preparing
to let this day go.

**AS I DO,
THANKS IS OFFERED
FOR
EVERY ACT OF
KINDNESS,
GENEROSITY
AND LOVE
I WAS PART OF
TODAY.**

I am grateful for what was learned,
improved upon...

Grateful,
also,
for the food I nourished
my Body Temple with,
the air breathed,
the water I drank
and bathed in,
the clothes worn,
home lived in as shelter,
the transportation
which allowed mobility
from one place
to another...

The blessings are so numerous
I cannot possibly single out
each one.

Whatever may have been
frustrating,
troublesome,
or,
lacking
in harmony,
I ask Divine Insight
and Guidance
to infuse me overnight
with
increased wisdom.

AS YOUR BELOVED CHILD,
I RECOGNIZE THAT
I AM NEVER
ALONE.

When I call,
Your responsiveness
is
unfailingly

present,
freeing
and blessed.

**MAY EVERY BEAUTIFUL BLESSING
TOMORROW BRINGS,
BE LOVED.**

How Does This Prayer Apply to Your Life Right Now?

What Emotions and Dreams Does This Bring Up for You?

How Would You Modify This Prayer in Your Own Words?

USING THIS PRAYER,
WHAT IS ONE STEP
YOU CAN DO
TO
TRANSFORM THE ABUSE
YOU'VE ENDURED?

WHO HAVE BEEN
YOUR MOST INSPIRING
TEACHERS IN THIS LIFETIME?
HOW MIGHT THEY RESPOND
TO THIS PRAYER?
WHAT WOULD THEY SHARE
TO SUPPORT YOUR
HEALING PROCESS?

Glossary

Blameshifting /Stonewalling:
It's when someone is caught doing
something wrong.
Blameshifting also happens
when a narcissistic personality
consciously decides to shift responsibility.

It is typical of their strong practice
of scapegoating others
refusing to consider empathetically
the impact
their behavior can have
on another's life.

Yet the person has ***no awareness that
something wrong has been done
or is in
total denial.***

Usually they will turn it around
and tell you:
- You are the cause of all their problems.
- You're trying to sabotage their happy life.
- You're trying to break up the relationship
and you just need some excuse.

- early childhood
- emotional,

730

physical,
psychological,
spiritual
trauma
often behave in ***extremely***
unreliable,
unpredictable,
illogical,
ways.

Often without malice because of
a lack of ***empathy***,
or the ability to think
about the ***consequences of their actions***,
they conduct themselves in ways
that tend to produce
apprehension,
anxiety,
lowered self-esteem
in the people
closest to them.

They often have grown up in such
chaotic,
addictive,
unstable

and dysfunctional
environments,
that
drama and nerve wracking
atmospheres
feel normal to them.

Though they may consciously wish
for serenity,
their actions tend toward causing
last minute emergencies and wreak havoc
with
plans,
dates
and commitments
making any sort of
happy,
stable
relationships
nearly impossible to maintain.

Cellular Memory:
Remembrance of every impression
and experience
is retained
within the trillions of cells
which form
our physical bodies.

Crazymaker, Drama King,
Drama Queen, Energy Vampire,
and
Narcissist:
These are people, who as a result of:
The phase of ***devaluing*** and ***excessively***
criticizing their prey begins,
through no fault of the victim
other than their own inability
to be aware enough
of the ***red flags***
which ***inevitably***
have been in front of them
all along.

Crazymaking:
Behavior which is evidenced by a lack of
valuing your
time,
needs,
or the needs of others
in the service

of somebody who feels entitled to:
• Come over whenever they want.
• Show up late or early
• Does not follow through on generous
and lavish promises.
• Violates all the healthy boundaries
which make for a good relationship.

Cognitive Dissonance
Cognitive Dissonance
happens when one knows
or desperately wants something to
be true
and discovers contrary evidence. It
is a process of trying to come
to make **inner peace**
with conflicting ideas.

Example: A man lavashes
great romantic attentions
on a woman
and seems like her soulmate,

733

yet she notices that he
lies,
exaggerates,
is not faithful,
so she has **cognitive dissonance**
because she wants to believe
that he's as wonderful
as she hopes he is.
The cognitive dissonance is caused
as **she struggles to convince herself**
that what she wants is within her grasp
with him,
versus the reality
of his
caricature defects.

Covert Narcissist :
A person whose dysfunction is difficult
to spot because the behavior is often limited
to one or two people
who have the unfortunate resemblance
(physically,
emotionally
or
energetically)
with the primary perpetrator
of emotional trauma
from the narcissist's childhood.
A covert narcissist can be extremely:
• charming
• bright
• witty
and

• often holds significant places of honor
in the community
• does wonderful, charitable work...
yet has a very dark side which can be
abusive to those who aggravate him,
or her.

The abusiveness seems so incongruous,
almost like a separate life
because the demeanor they display
outside of
one,
or,
two
people
is usually so
wonderful,
helpful
and
generous.

Delusions of Grandeur:
Completely unrealistic flights of fancy
inflating an individual's
status,
abilities,
mission in life

to a virtually impossible level
to achieve.

Elevation Phase / Love Bombing:
This transpires during the initial weeks
up to approximately three months,
when a narcissistic individual
seeks to seduce his,
or her,
prey
with overwhelming amounts of:
- attention
- approval
- compliments
- lavish gifts
- poetry
- flowers
- sexual prowess...

and/or other means
to make him,
or her,
feel that life will only
become even better
as long as they are
together.

Usually by three to six months at the most,
there will be a reversal
on the part
of the
narcissist.

The phase of ***devaluing*** and ***excessively
criticizing*** their prey begins,
through no fault of the victim
other than their own inability
to be aware enough
of the ***red flags***
which ***inevitably***
have been in front of them
all along.

Elitism :
It is based on the concept
of one person believing
they are somehow
"better and far superior"
to another.

It often manifests as
a condescending attitude,
an *"us"* versus *"them"*
approach.

Frequently it is a cover
for a deep-seated sense
of inadequacy and fraudulence.

Empaths:
Empaths have a great capacity to
feel, and *identify* strongly
with narcissistic manipulators
who mistake their
kindness for *weakness.*
They are natural born targets
for the ability of a narcissistic personality
to immediately identify someone
who's
warmth,
intelligence,
and
benevolent
nature
they can seduce and then eventually
abandon
and/or torture.

737

Entitlement:
This is an attitude or condition of
mind and heart which makes
people feel
that they are due
special treatment,
convenience,
comfort,
pay,
amenities,
titles
and other advantages
which set them apart
from the rest of society
who they often consider
to be
"mere peons",
"pawns",
"trash"
and
"tools".

Energy Vampires:
People who are so compromised to fill their
own
emotional,
psychological

and
spiritual
needs,
that the suck
the **strength** and **life force**
from
family,
friends,
coworkers,
schoolmates,
lovers,
and
anyone else
they can find,
"the battery charge supply of attention
they crave."
Like any other addict,
the energy vampires are insatiable
in their neediness.
This need for attention,
whether positive or negative,
tends to become more pronounced
with age.

Flying Monkey:
This refers to
some of *the people*
who are often enlisted by a
crazymaker,
narcissist
and energy vampire
to spread
gossip,
exaggerations
and outright lies
about an individual
the narcissist has been using,
and is about to *discard*,
or, *has discarded.*

Gaslighting
Gaslighting is deliberately
trying to make someone doubt
the truth
of their own knowing
by
deceiving,
lying,
exaggerating,
insulting,
the intelligence
of the victim.

738

Gray Rock Technique
An escape strategy
used by the prey of a narcissist
to make him or her
loose interest
to leave him or her alone.
This is a frequently successful method
of letting the separation
from the narcissist
be the narcissist's own idea.
This method can save
the narcissist's prey
a great deal of
aggravation,
slander,
sarcasm,
financial
and
psychological
abuse.

who's
warmth,
intelligence,
and
benevolent
nature
they can seduce and then eventually
abandon
and/or torture.

Hoovering
Hoovering is an attempt
by the narcissist to
reunite romantically,
as a
friend,
business partner,
a group member,
an employee,
an advisor,
with the promise that everything
will be better,
positively different
in every wonderful way.
Overture or hoovering can come within
days,
weeks,
or **years**
of when

the *separation discarding breakup happened.*

BEWARE OF HOOVERING

because there's usually no internal shifts for the better!

Beverly Banov Brown, M.S.,

often referred to as,
"The Poet of Prayer,"
is internationally known as an **Intuitive
Healer/Personal** and **Business Life Coach**.
Also an Interfaith Chaplain, and
Founding Director of the
**LightBridge Interfaith Prayer
Community**,
which has provided free,
non-denominational prayer since 1997,
her video talks on social media have reached
well over one million viewers.

Beverly's **YouTube channel**, has 200 videos
where she discusses such topics as,
**Codependency,
Narcissistic Abuse,
Authentic Dating,
Inner Peace,
Joyful Marriage,
Vanishing Twin Syndrome**
and **How to Thrive Despite
the Challenges of Our World.**

Beverly is also the
Founder of
Your Transcendence Now Academy,
(currently under development) an online

learning center featuring extensive
experiential business,
and **relationship,** classes.

Author of the **Windflyer** Series, and the
Prayer Companion Journal Series,

**A Prayer Companion Journal for the
Inspired Entrepreneur's Soul,**

**A Prayer Companion Journal for the
Spiritual Seeker's Soul,**

**A Prayer Companion Journal for the
Recovering Codependent's Soul,** etc...

Also a prolific watercolorist,
Beverly coaches an international clientele,
by phone, at her office
in the Tampa Bay area of Florida.

Feel free to get in touch with
**Beverly Banov Brown, M.S.,
with suggestions for new
Prayer Companion Journals,
or,
requests for
Coaching Consultations**
at
coachhq@gmail.com

Made in the USA
Monee, IL
10 December 2020

52112242R00411